Peter Atkinson is Chancellor and Residentiary Canon of Chichester Cathedral, and a former Principal of Chichester Theological College. He has also served in parishes in south London, Surrey, Bath and Sussex.

Friendship and the Body of Christ

Peter Atkinson

First published in Great Britain in 2004 by
Society for Promoting Christian Knowledge
36 Causton Street
London SW1P 4ST

The publisher and author acknowledge with thanks permission
to reproduce extracts from the following:
'If', by Rudyard Kipling, by permission of A P Watt on behalf of the
National Trust for Places of Historic Interest or Natural Beauty.

Scripture quotations are from the Revised Standard Version of the
Bible, Copyright © 1946, 1952 and 1971; and from the New Revised
Standard Version of the Bible, copyright © 1989 by the Division of
Christian Education of the National Council of the Churches of
Christ in the USA. Used by permission. All rights reserved.

British Library Cataloguing-in-Publication Data
A catalogue record for this book is available from the British Library

ISBN 0-281-05693-5

1 3 5 7 9 10 8 6 4 2

Typeset by Avocet Typeset, Chilton, Aylesbury, Bucks
Printed in Great Britain by Bookmarque Ltd, Croydon, Surrey

To the 'Cell':
Adrian, Charles, David, Stephen
and in memory of Trevor

Contents

Preface   ix

1 I Have Called You Friends   1

2 Friendship and the Old Testament   10

3 Friendship in the Classical Tradition   16

4 St Augustine to St Aelred: A Developing Tradition   23

5 Sworn Friends   33

6 Men and Women   44

7 Friendship and Homosexuality   53

8 Are You My Friend?   65

Notes   71

Further Reading   79

Index   83

Preface

'Are you my friend?'
'I'm not friends with you any more.'
'Let's make friends.'

If these phrases remind us of the playground, that tells us more about ourselves and our casual adult approach to friendship than it does about our children, who have preserved a more ancient sense of the form and ceremony of being friends. As modern adults we tend to class friendship as part of our 'private' lives, together with our leisure and our religion. Christians of earlier centuries lived in a different culture, in which the private and public spheres were less demarcated, and friendship was understood both to belong to the structure of society and to be a proper subject for spiritual reflection. They knew that friendship was sanctified by the example of Christ, and that in his grace two people could discover a deep 'spiritual friendship', which was sometimes described in sacramental terms. They would not have understood the dismissive phrase, 'just good friends'. Such friendship might exist between men, between women, or between a man and a woman. It was sometimes expressed in passionate language and intimate behaviour, which our more private culture would find surprising.

Where such formalized, 'sacramental' friendships existed between people of the same sex, it naturally occurs to us to ask whether they were 'homosexual'. The difficulty of applying terms such as 'homosexual' or 'gay' to different and earlier cultures is explored in David Greenberg's *The Construction of Homosexuality* (1988); nonetheless the celebration in earlier Christian ages of formal same-sex friendship suggests a road forward for the Church today. In his book, *The Friend* (2003), to which I refer a good deal, the late Alan Bray suggests we can 'see in the past ways of transcending – with integrity on all sides – the looming confrontation that is still with us between Christianity and homosexuality without the damaging conflict on which it seems bent'. I hope this book might contribute a little to the limitation of that damage.

This book began as a series of lectures given in Chichester Cathedral, and I am grateful to those who heard them and took part in subsequent discussion. I am grateful too to my wife and children for their tolerant enthusiasm, and to my brother Bishop David Atkinson for his critical encouragement. The opportunity to read again the works of Sir Richard Southern has reminded me of the happy years when I was an undergraduate of St John's College, Oxford, and he its distinguished president.

The dedication of the book records my debt to a group of friends, with whom I have enjoyed the kind of friendship that St Augustine evokes in Book 4 of the *Confessions*: 'to make conversation, to share a joke ... to read together well-written books; to share in trifling and in serious matters, to disagree though without animosity ... and in the very rarity of disagreement to find the salt of normal harmony'. The author of Ecclesiasticus tells us that 'faithful friends are a sturdy shelter'. I am grateful to this particular shelter that has stood firm for a quarter of a century and more.

1

I Have Called You Friends

The lamps are lit in the upper room, but the air is fraught with foreboding. Jesus and his disciples are at their last supper together. He has worried them by taking the servant's part and washing their feet, and confused them by saying that they cannot follow where he is going. His speech is riddling, as it often is. None of them doubts that the opposition is mustering somewhere near. Judas has just vanished into the night. It is in this tense atmosphere that Jesus turns to them and says:

> 'This is my commandment, that you love one another as I have loved you. No one has greater love than this, to lay down one's life for one's friends. You are my friends if you do what I command you. I do not call you servants any longer, because the servant does not know what the master is doing; but I have called you friends, because I have made known to you everything that I have heard from my Father.'[1]

Here the fourth evangelist brings together many of the themes of his Gospel. Right at the outset, he tells us that 'no one has ever seen God. It is God the only Son, who is close to the Father's heart, who has made him known'[2]. The mission of the Son, then, is to make the Father known. Those to whom he does so are raised from the level of servants and disciples to that of friends. Upon these confused and frightened disciples, uncertain of their role and doubtful of what Jesus has in mind, he confers the privilege that Scripture ascribed only to Abraham and Moses: of being the friends of God.

St John wrote in Greek; and the Greek word for friend is *philos,* with its accompanying abstract noun *philia* (friendship) and verb *phileo* (to love as a friend). St John also uses another set of words, the verb *agapao* and the noun *agape,* which also mean 'love'. In some contexts it may be possible to sense a difference between these two sets of words; C. S. Lewis drew a sharp distinction between them in his book *The Four Loves*. There he distinguished *philia,* the ordinary Greek word for friendship (the word for instance that Aristotle used to discuss the idea), from *agape,* the gracious, disinterested love that God reveals to us in Christ, the love that St Paul celebrates in 1 Corinthians 13. In the Johannine writings, however, it is hard to distinguish them. There are passages, such as the one quoted above, in which both words are clearly used interchangeably. St John does not have a special word for the love or friendship of God: he presses into theological service the ordinary categories of human relationship.

All four evangelists write their Gospels with some idea of the Church implicit in the story they tell. For St Mark, the Church is implicit in the Twelve to whom Christ imparts the secret of the kingdom of heaven. For St Matthew, there is the more developed idea of the followers of Jesus as the new Israel, the new people of God, of whom the Twelve are the twelve 'judges'. In the Acts of the Apostles, St Luke describes the origin of the Church as the community of disciples upon whom God pours out the Holy Spirit. St John adopts a different approach from any of these. He directs our attention to the way Jesus calls his disciples and forms them into a group of friends. While St Matthew gives us the Sermon on the Mount with its command to love even our enemies, and St Luke gives us the parable of the Good Samaritan who puts that love into practice, St John seems to close the shutters and draw the curtains and concentrate on the love shown within the group of disciples. 'Love one another', Jesus says to them, 'as I have loved you.'[3] 'We know that we have passed from death to life', writes St John in his First Epistle, 'because we love the brethren.'[4] The group of disciples, the 'brethren', is the context in which, in Johannine theology, the love of God is put into practice; and it is the love of God celebrated within the close-knit circle of disciples that authenticates for the fourth evangelist the truth of Christianity.

Generally we read St John read through a haze of memories of the other Gospels; and it may come as a shock to realize how restricted a framework is offered by St John for the exercise of 'brotherly' love. Even the well-known words, 'No one has greater love than this, to lay down one's life for one's friends', leave us wondering whether there might not be a still greater love, in laying down our life for those who are *not* our friends. This, however, is to mistake the evangelist's purpose. The Christian community for which St John is writing is evidently a fragile and embattled group, beset on all sides by betrayal, repression and persecution. (This is even clearer in the three Johannine Epistles – clearer still if we include the Apocalypse.) The possibility of betrayal is a main Johannine theme.[5] It is a community under pressure, liable to fragmentation; and the evangelist tells the story of Jesus and his disciples in such a way as to encourage the Church of his own time. The miracle of grace, as St John unfolds it, is not so much the miracle of the Good Samaritan, who sacrificially tends the ancestral enemy, but the miracle of friendship within a group of people under pressure to break and run. St Luke tells the story of the 'wideness of God's mercy' that reaches harlot and Pharisee, thief and tax-collector. St John, however, tells the complementary story of the depth of God's mercy that can forge such bonds of love and loyalty within the group that they are prepared even to lay down their lives for one another.

And so St John dramatizes his Gospel as the story of a group of friends. He is interested, not only in how the disciples are related to Jesus, but how they relate to each other. In the Fourth Gospel the disciples converse with each other, which they don't, by and large, in the other Gospels. Andrew tells Simon that he has found the Messiah;[6] Philip passes on the message to Nathanael;[7] Thomas says to the others, 'Let us also go that we may die with him;[8] Philip tells Andrew about the Greeks who would see Jesus:[9] these interactions are all characteristic of St John's dramatic art. And then there are the great haunting images from the closing scenes of the drama: the household of Lazarus, Martha and Mary, all of whom 'Jesus loved';[10] the last supper when the beloved disciple leans on the breast of Jesus, and Peter bids him ask Jesus who the betrayer might be;[11] the foot of the cross where we find the beloved disciple and the Lord's mother;[12] the empty tomb to which Peter and the beloved disciple run;[13] and the moving epilogue beside the Sea of Galilee, with Jesus and Peter walking side by side, and the beloved disciple behind them, when Peter turns to say, 'Lord, what about this man?'[14] These are all scenes in which friendships are formed, celebrated, damaged or repaired.

All friendships carry the risk of betrayal, and so St John develops from the outset the figure of the traitor. This is where the restricted scope of the Fourth Gospel touches on matters of life and death in ways the broad scope of St Luke does not. St John and his hearers, like Jesus and the first disciples, had been brought up to sing those heartbreaking words of the Psalter: 'All who hate me whisper together about me; they imagine the worst for me. Even my bosom friend in whom I trusted, who ate of my bread, has lifted the heel against me.'[15] Or again, 'It is not enemies who taunt me – I could bear that; it is not adversaries who deal insolently with me – I could hide from them. But it is you, my equal, my companion, my familiar friend, with whom I kept pleasant company; we walked in the house of God with the throng.'[16] And so St John weaves the story of Judas into his narrative, preparing the ground by speaking in general terms of those who loved darkness rather than light because their deeds were evil,[17] and then describing the last supper at which the hands of Jesus and Judas meet in the dish of bread. His familiar friend and companion, who ate of his bread and with whom he had walked in the house of God, had lifted the heel against him.

'What you are going to do,' says Jesus, in the intimacy of that moment of betrayal, 'do quickly.' So Judas goes out: *en de nux*, says the Evangelist: 'and it was night'.[18]

Parallel to the figure of Judas is the enigmatic figure of the 'beloved disciple'. This figure has traditionally been identified with the evangelist himself, and in turn with John, the brother of James, the son of Zebedee. There is no need to debate the matter here, which has found no unanimity among scholars, ancient or modern. All we need to notice is that the evangelist singles out one disciple for a particular part to play in the closing chapters of the Gospel, whom he does not name but whom he calls 'the disciple whom Jesus loved'. This disciple is mentioned for the first time only at the last supper, where he leans upon the breast of Jesus, and is close enough to ask him who the traitor is. As Jesus is also close enough to speak confidentially to Judas, the picture the evangelist paints is that of Jesus flanked by the 'beloved disciple' on one side and the traitor on the other: a picture of friendship both sealed and broken at the supper table. The 'beloved disciple' is later given the task of providing the Lord's mother with a home, and the honour of reaching the empty tomb first on hearing the news from Mary Magdalen; and it is his personal destiny which occupies the closing words of the epilogue of the Gospel.[19] It may be that he is the same figure as the one who, together with Peter, follows Jesus into the court of the high priest after his arrest,[20] in which case he is the figure of the loyal friend who does not betray him (like Judas) or deny him (like Peter) or desert him (like the others). In him are concentrated both the joys and the griefs of faithful friendship.

The figure of the 'beloved disciple' has another aspect. The evangelist goes out of his way to say that at the last supper he 'lay close to the breast' of Jesus. Of course, this reflects the first-century custom of reclining at table, the posture adopted on formal occasions. But the picture of the disciple reclining in the breast of Jesus says two things. First, it is a picture of remarkable intimacy. It emphasizes how not only the Passover but every meal establishes a sacred fellowship among those who take part. And it reminds us that the gospel story was born in a culture in which close physical contact was possible between friends even in formal contexts. But there is more to it than that. There is an unmistakable echo here of St John's prologue. For there we are told that from all eternity the Son is 'in the breast' or 'the bosom' of the Father.[21] That is where the eternal Son resides, and he resides there still even as he goes about his mission to humankind: 'the Word of God proceeding forth,' as St Thomas Aquinas put it, 'yet leaving not his Father's side'.[22] His mission is to make his Father known. He who has seen him has seen the Father. So the disciple who rests intimately in the bosom of Jesus also rests in the bosom of the Father, even as Jesus does. The picture of the beloved disciple leaning back against Jesus at the supper table is more than a snapshot of first-century table customs: it is a glimpse of our eternal destiny, to rest in the heart of Jesus, and so rest in the heart of God who has called us to be his friends.

The other disciples of Jesus are neither wholly traitorous (like Judas) nor wholly faithful (like the 'beloved disciple'). And so between the two, we are given (as in the other Gospels) the figure of Peter, which the fourth evangelist develops in particular ways of his own. It is in the epilogue (chapter 21) that we have the unforgettable scene in which Jesus interrogates Peter three times. Here St John uses both *agape* and *philia*; and here perhaps, in close proximity and great dramatic intensity, it may be possible to distinguish them. Archbishop William Temple put it like this: 'Simon, son of John, do you love me more than these?' 'Yes, Lord, you know that I am your friend.' 'Simon, son of John, do you love me?' 'Yes, Lord, you know that I am your friend.' 'Simon, son of John, are you my friend?' 'Lord, you know all things; you know that I am your friend.'[23] Perhaps Peter cannot quite dare say that he 'loves' Jesus; he offers friendship as a humbler alternative. Perhaps, too, Jesus is content to take up Peter's humbler word in his third question, filling it with all the profundity that he has already given it, and therefore raises Peter's humble words to a level Peter dare not give them. Here, at any rate, is the picture of friendship restored.

The last of St John's chief *dramatis personae* is Mary Magdalen. In the Fourth Gospel she appears among the women gathered near the cross, and later is given the privileged role of the first disciple to see the risen Lord. If we read St John in the light of St Luke (and there is much common ground between them) then it is legitimate to recall St Luke's picture of Mary Magdalen as the woman from whom the Lord expelled seven demons. In any case, we can tell from the way that St John tells his story that Mary had some deep and particular personal devotion to Jesus: she alone takes the trouble and the risk to linger near his grave.[24] And when she meets him and mistakes him for the gardener and then realizes who he is, she longs (naturally enough) to embrace him. The Lord's reply (*Me mou haptou* in Greek, *Noli me tangere* in Latin) is difficult to capture in English: something like 'do not cling to me' or 'do not hold on to me' is best. Much ink has been spilt in explaining the words. We need to remember that they do not stand on their own: Jesus goes on, 'for I have not yet ascended to my Father'. That echoes his words at the last supper: 'If I do not go away the Advocate will not come to you.'[25] The Lord must withdraw his bodily presence in order that his spiritual presence may be with them. So Jesus is not *recoiling* from Mary; he is gently explaining that she cannot cling to his bodily presence any more. In any case, she has a task to do: she must tell the disciples of the resurrection. As later Christian writers put it, she is to be *apostola apostolorum*: the apostle to the apostles. So Jesus 'makes known' to Mary 'what he has received from his Father'; she too is among those whom he has called to be his friends.

More than fifty years ago, the Professor of Romance Languages at Yale, Erich Auerbach, published a monumental book called *Mimesis: The Representation of Reality in Western Literature.* It is a study of works of literature drawn from many ages and cultures, and how their authors portray their scenes and characters realistically. In his study of the Gospels he remarks how, compared to classical literature, the evangelists adopt a radically new dramatic style. In classical antiquity, high tragedy was a style appropriate to the nobly born; the common people served as extras, crowds or comic relief. But in the Gospels, people like Peter from humble backgrounds enact a tragic and heroic part.

> Of course [writes Auerbach], this mingling of styles is not dictated by an artistic purpose. On the contrary, it was rooted from the beginning in the character of Jewish-Christian literature; it was graphically and harshly dramatized through God's incarnation in a human being of the humblest social station, through his existence on earth amid humble everyday people and conditions, and through his Passion which, judged by earthly standards, was ignominious.[26]

Auerbach's thesis might well be applied to the representation of friendship in the Fourth Gospel. Friendship, in the writings of Cicero (for instance) is a rare, refined and noble quality. Only three or four pairs of friends, he says, have been celebrated in literature.[27] Yet St John not only establishes friendship as a central theological image and makes it a principal metaphor for expressing the relationship of redeemed humanity with God: he depicts this 'noble' gift of friendship as being conferred upon a circle of Galilean fishermen and tax-collectors. And this both sanctifies 'ordinary' human friendship and transforms it. If the 'ordinary' friendship of two people can serve as an image of the relationship of God and humankind, then that 'ordinary' friendship is a very extraordinary thing indeed, and that 'ordinary' friendship has potentialities that those two 'ordinary' people may not have dreamt of. Even in its 'ordinary' state, there is something godlike about it.

The Church, so St John tells us, is the place where God enables people to become friends. Relations between the baptized are not determined by the things that determine so much of our personal relationships: sex, politics, economics. St John puts it like this in his prologue: those who receive the Word made flesh are born, 'not of blood or of the will of the flesh or of the will of man, but of God'.[28] Neither race, nor sexuality, nor the conventions of human society, says St John, determine the way we live out our friendship with God and, in him, with one another. And therein lie a gift, an opportunity and a challenge.

2

Friendship and the Old Testament

The early readers of the Fourth Gospel had two sources upon which to draw if they wished to think about friendship. They are the Scriptures of the Old Testament, which we will consider in this chapter, and the writings of the classical authors, which we will look at in the next.

The rewards and risks of human friendship are a theme that runs through the 'wisdom' books of the Old Testament. Its most extended treatment is to be found in chapter 6 of the Wisdom of Jesus son of Sirach (or Ecclesiasticus – one of the books in the Old Testament Apocrypha, dating from the second century BC):

> Pleasant speech multiplies friends,
>> and a gracious tongue multiplies courtesies.
> Let those who are friendly with you be many,
>> but let your advisers be one in a thousand.
> When you gain friends, gain them through testing,
>> and do not trust them hastily.
> For there are friends who are such when it suits them,
>> but they will not stand by you in time of trouble.
> And there are friends who change into enemies,
>> and tell of the quarrel to your disgrace.
> And there are friends who sit at your table,
>> but they will not stand by you in time of trouble.
> When you are prosperous, they become your second self,
>> and lord it over your servants;

but if you are brought low, they turn against you,
　　and hide themselves from you.
Keep away from your enemies,
　　and be on guard with your friends.[1]

Despite all these cautionary remarks, the author finally lets himself go:

Faithful friends are a sturdy shelter:
　　whoever finds one has found a treasure.
Faithful friends are beyond price;
　　no amount can balance their worth.
Faithful friends are life-saving medicine;
　　and those who fear the Lord will find them.[2]

Sirach returns to the theme in other passages. Loyalty to friends is valued: 'Do not abandon old friends, for new ones cannot equal them.'[3] Friends may be estranged or even become enemies, but with true friendship reconciliation is always possible: 'Even if you draw your sword against a friend, do not despair, for there is a way back.'[4] Is it better to be without friends at all? Not at all: 'I have no friends' is the confession of a fool.[5] Friendship stops one from behaving badly: 'Be ashamed . . . of unjust dealing before your partner or your friend.'[6]

In the Book of Proverbs, we find friendship compared and contrasted with kinship: 'a friend loves at all times, and kinsfolk are born to share adversity'; 'some friends play at friendship but a true friend sticks closer than one's kin'.[7] As in Sirach, prosperity may betray one into false friendships: 'everyone is a friend to a giver of gifts'.[8] The words of a true friend are to be valued even if they hurt: 'faithful are the wounds of a friend'.[9] In the Book of Job, on the other hand, the advice of well-intentioned but foolish friends is excoriated by both Job and God.[10]

The 'wisdom' books are humane, pragmatic and platitudinous. They reflect a perennial concern with the risks and rewards of friendship that can be paralleled in many cultures.

We will hear it again in Cicero. We hear it in Polonius' advice to Laertes:

> Those friends thou hast, and their adoption tried,
> Grapple them to thy soul with hoops of steel;
> But do not dull thy palm with entertainment
> Of each new-hatch'd, unfledg'd courage. Beware
> Of entrance to a quarrel; but, being in,
> Bear't that th'opposed may beware of thee.
> Give every man thy ear, but few thy voice;
> Take each man's censure, but reserve thy judgement.[11]

We hear it in Kipling's 'If – '

> If neither foes nor loving friends can hurt you,
> If all men count with you, but none too much,[12]

This is a wisdom rooted in a world of practically minded men, not much given to theological speculation, but where the trust of comrades and colleagues is given and withheld, confidences are made and broken, reputations are damaged and defended, a helping hand proffered or withdrawn.

The most famous friendship of the Old Testament is that of David and Jonathan. Following David's victory over Goliath, we read that 'the soul of Jonathan was bound to the soul of David, and Jonathan loved him as his own soul ... Then Jonathan made a covenant with David because he loved him as his own soul.'[13] Later on we read that 'Saul's son Jonathan took great delight in David'.[14] As Saul's jealousy increases, Jonathan both warns David and intercedes on behalf of David with Saul, and later arranges David's escape from Saul's court. Jonathan again 'makes a covenant with the house of David', and he 'made David swear again by his love for him; for he loved him as he loved his own life'.[15] As they take their leave of each other, 'they kissed each other and wept with each other'.[16] They did not meet again; both Saul and Jonathan fell in battle against the Philistines on Mount Gilboa, prompting David's lament for them:

> Saul and Jonathan, beloved and lovely!
>> In life and in death they were not divided;
> they were swifter than eagles,
>> they were stronger than lions . . .
> How the mighty have fallen
>> in the midst of the battle!
> Jonathan lies slain upon your high places.
>> I am distressed for you, my brother Jonathan;
> greatly beloved were you to me;
>> your love to me was wonderful,
>> passing the love of women.[17]

Later on, David, now king, is concerned to make provision for Jonathan's crippled son Mephibosheth, restoring to him the confiscated lands of his grandfather Saul, and inviting him to eat at his own table.[18]

There are two critical issues in the story of David and Jonathan. One is whether the 'love' between the two men is primarily a personal relationship or a political one. The other is whether a sexual relationship is implied by the words of David's lament. While the story has generally been received as one of the warm mutual affection of two young warriors, some recent commentators have emphasized the political dimension of their 'covenant'. 'In the ancient Near East, "love" terminology belonged to the language of political discourse, and many of the statements made about Jonathan's love for David are charged with political overtones,' writes P. Kyle McCarter in The Anchor Bible; though he agrees that 'there was also a warm intimacy between the two men'.[19] This is an issue we shall find recurring in the history of friendship. As we shall see, the idea of friendship as a purely personal and therefore essentially private relationship is a modern one. Until a change of attitude and custom came over Europe in the eighteenth century, friendships were felt to belong to the public sphere; and the friendships of princes could not fail to be politically significant. The title of the 'King's Friends' was applied to the confidential counsellors of the English crown. But if 'private' friendship is a modern concept, so also is the attempt to separate the personal from the public in ancient friendship. The fact that David's alliance with Jonathan had political significance does not mean that his lamentation after the battle of Mount Gilboa was the less sincere and heart-rending. Indeed, the interweaving of the personal and the political elements in the 'Court History' of David is part of the consummate narrative skill of the author.[20]

Is it a story of homosexual love? For some, it is self-evident: Schroer and Staubli in *Samuel and Kings: A Feminist Companion to the Bible*, for instance, write of 'the assumption which the text compels one to make, namely, that it speaks of a homosexual relationship'.[21] Other commentators consider it impossible that the story should have survived the condemnation of Leviticus; still others do not venture into the discussion. The reading of ancient narratives for evidence of what we would call a homosexual relationship is a difficult one, and a question to which we shall return in Chapter 5, when we shall have more examples to consider. Suffice it to say at this point that the phrase 'homosexual relationship' begs too many modern questions of a text three thousand years old; such a text cannot 'compel' one to make any 'assumptions' one way or another.

The image of friendship is occasionally used in the Old Testament as a metaphor for the relationship of humanity to God, but it is treated as a rare and wholly exceptional privilege. Only Abraham and Moses are individually described as God's friends. In the prophecy of Isaiah, God addresses the people as 'the offspring of Abraham my friend'.[22] In Exodus, we read that God spoke to Moses 'face to face as a man speaks to his friend';[23] we can compare this with the tribute paid to Moses at the end of Deuteronomy that 'never had there arisen a prophet in Israel like Moses, whom the Lord knew face to face'.[24] If friendship is here used as a metaphor to describe the relationship of a human being to God, it only underlines the exceptional spiritual stature of Abraham the father of the nation, and Moses the liberator and lawgiver. And if friendship with God is equated with seeing him 'face to face', that further emphasizes its rarity, for in the Old Testament a face-to-face encounter with God usually means annihilation.[25] The first suggestion that God's friendship might be conferred more generally comes in the Wisdom of Solomon (in the Old Testament Apocrypha, dating from the first century BC). Here the author offers a hymn in praise of wisdom, echoing a theme in both Job and Proverbs. 'In every generation,' he writes, 'she passes into holy souls and makes them friends of God and prophets.'[26] We are coming closer to St John's conception of the Word who reveals God to chosen human beings and calls them his friends. That is also connected in the Fourth Gospel with the idea of 'seeing' God: those whom the Son calls into friendship are those who (in seeing the Son) see the Father also, and those who (like the beloved disciple) rest in the bosom of the Son, even as the Son rests in the bosom of the Father. Vision, intimacy and friendship together form a cluster of images that run throughout the Bible.

3

Friendship in the Classical Tradition

The Greek philosophers formed the intellectual climate of the world in which Christianity developed, and profoundly influenced the development of Christian thought. The influence began in the pre-Christian period, as the Jews were increasingly dispersed across the Mediterranean world. Passages in the Wisdom of Solomon reflect this meeting of cultures. Not surprisingly, the New Testament authors display various degrees of classical learning. St Paul, while deriding the 'wisdom of the Greeks' in 1 Corinthians 1, can still write a passage such as that beginning 'whatever is true, whatever is honourable, whatever is just, whatever is pure',[1] which echoes the language of Stoicism. The author of Acts portrays Paul as being at home on the Areopagus and quoting the Stoic poets.[2] And St John, as we have seen, adopts the image of the Word, the *Logos*, which is close to Hellenistic Judaism.[3] Some early Christian writers denounced the idea of clothing Christian truth in the garments of pagan philosophers ('What has Athens to do with Jerusalem?' Tertullian in the second century indignantly demanded); but it was Athens that had created the intellectual currency of the classical world, and if Christians were to communicate with their contemporaries there was no other ground on which they could do so.

It is not surprising, then, that Christian authors took up the theme of friendship, that plays so prominent a part in St John's Gospel, and explored it in terms of what the classical authors had already had to say about it. Plato wrote about friendship, and so did Aristotle, and in the century before Christ the Roman author Cicero wrote a treatise on it that would echo, as we shall see, down the Christian centuries. Whether or not the first readers of St John's Gospel had read the classical authors themselves, it was those authors who shaped the mindset of the time.

Plato's principal treatment of friendship is the *Lysis* (written *c.* 380 BC). Plato's dialogues are dramatic presentations of the wisdom of Socrates, teased out in conversation among groups of men or boys. The all-male cast is part of the dramatic setting, though no doubt it reflects the character of the age. In the *Lysis*, Socrates is made to engage in a discussion of the nature of friendship (*philia*) and pretends not to be able to define it; indeed, he confesses to never having found a true friend for himself at all. This literary device enables Plato to touch on many of the themes that we shall find recurring in later treatments of the subject. Friendship is reciprocal: it cannot exist one-sidedly; that much is clear. So, asks Socrates, is friendship the mutual attraction of likes or of opposites? If the former, this can apply only to the good, for the bad must be at enmity with each other and cannot form true friendships. Yet if the good person is by definition morally self-sufficient, how can they be in need of friends? On the other hand, if friendship is the attraction of opposites, as Hesiod had already maintained, then the good would make friends only of the bad. 'May not all these notions of friendship be erroneous?' Socrates asks ruefully at one point. Eventually he comes round to the theory that, after all, friendship must be a desire for that which is congenial, but he allows that theory only in the case of the good person – a theory he has already refuted. Plato makes Socrates, the friendliest of men, conclude the dialogue by admitting that he has not been able to discover what it is to be a friend.

If the *Lysis* is his only direct treatment of friendship, there is much more in Plato's work that has conditioned later Christian reflection on the subject. The central theme of Plato's philosophy is that the physical, observable world around us is but a mirror, a shadow, an imperfect image of the unseen and eternal world. Change and decay are characteristic of the observable world: permanence and changelessness mark the world that is unseen. The task of the spiritual or moral or philosophical life is to approach as closely as possible to the contemplation of these perfect realities or 'forms'; and in order to do this we use their various copies in this world as stepping stones, so to speak, to the unseen world. One such 'form' is beauty: to approach the contemplation of perfect beauty, we must both contemplate and pass beyond the contemplation of beautiful things in this world. And the word Plato uses for this contemplative activity is 'love' (*eros*). *Eros*, of course, is not sex. For Plato, *eros* is the desire for beauty. A beautiful human being (especially, for Plato, a beautiful young man) could move the heart towards the contemplation of the eternal beauty of which that person was a reflection. Lust, on the other hand, is an irrational distraction from that contemplative quest. In his earlier dialogues, Plato endorsed the *mores* of the time and saw positive good in a physical homosexual relationship, especially between a teacher and a pupil; but by the time he wrote his last work, the *Laws,* he had come to think that sexual love was so much of an irrational distraction that it could be justified only on the grounds of procreation.[4] This marks the beginning of one of several long threads of sexual renunciation that run throughout subsequent Christian history.

We have to be careful how we use the word 'platonic'. Marsilio Ficino in the fifteenth century was apparently the one who coined the phrase 'platonic love' to mean a love that is 'spiritual' (in the unbiblical sense of 'disembodied'). It has come down to us to mean any non-sexual relationship. But Plato's love, even when stripped of physical expression, is passionate, erotic; it is 'being in love'. It is Dante's love for Beatrice that reaches from hell to paradise. It is the unrequited love that Socrates inspires in Alcibiades, which Plato celebrates in the

Symposium. Desire is the essential component of 'platonic' love.

Aristotle (384–322 BC) devotes two out of the ten books of the *Nicomachean Ethics* to friendship, but none to sex, which says a lot about his scale of priorities. No one, he says at the beginning of Book 8, would choose a friendless existence for all the other 'goods' in the world; 'friendship being a necessity of human nature is a good thing and a precious'.[5] He repeats the great platitudes we have already met in the 'wisdom' literature: 'In poverty and all the other misfortunes of life the thoughts of men turn to their friends as their one refuge.'[6] Friendship is a kind of virtue, he says, returning to the point at which Socrates found himself faltering: 'some even believe that to be a friend you must also be a good man'. And so Aristotle begins to distinguish levels of friendship: there is the friendship of two people who are useful to each other; and there is the friendship of those who are amused by each other's company. Neither of these is bad, but they fall short of the friendship of those who love one other for their own sake.[7] This is the truly virtuous friendship, the friendship of two good people who love the good in each other, unconditioned by time, circumstance or self-interest. Such friendships imply a certain equality; but Aristotle goes on to discuss the possibility of friendship between those who are *not* (according to the standards of his time) equal: parents and children, husbands and wives, rulers and subjects.[8] Here friendship becomes possible where the two partners, admittedly unequal to one another, each make their *proportionate* contribution to the relationship. (Aristotle's inclusion of marriage as a kind of friendship would have a lasting influence on the Christian tradition.) Even so, says Aristotle, there are limits to what is possible: the king cannot really be friends with his subjects, and it goes without saying that 'between God and man there can be no friendship'.[9] Reverting to the question of friendship as the attraction of likes or opposites, Aristotle firmly concludes that 'the good man feels towards his friend as he feels towards himself – for a friend is a second self'.[10] He goes on to discuss some practical matters: the competing claims of different friends (not easy; we must do the best we can),[11] the circumstances in which a friendship may be broken off (if the 'friend' turns out to be a person of bad character; but even so, the memory of past intimacy imposes the obligation to salvage what one can of the relationship);[12] how many friends should a person have? (not too many, or intimacy becomes impossible).[13]

For Aristotle, friendship is the foundation of civic virtue. The same classification that Aristotle makes of friendship in the *Nicomachean Ethics* can be traced out in his treatment of the city in the *Politics*. The city enables people to live together not only usefully (corresponding to the lowest level of friendship, that of practical co-operation), but also pleasurably (corresponding to the second level of friendship) and virtuously (corresponding to the ideal of perfect friendship). Given that Aristotle has already laid down that a person should cultivate no more friendships than can develop into intimacy, it follows that there is a clear difference in kind between personal and civic friendship. The idea that the virtues of friendship should be part of public as well as private life would survive in Christian thinking, as we shall see; it distinguishes both the classical and Christian traditions of friendship from their modern counterparts.

Cicero, who died in 43 BC, was not so much an original philosopher as an eloquent communicator. He described his task as 'teaching philosophy to speak Latin' – in other words, to make Greek philosophy familiar to the Latin-speaking world. His treatise on friendship, *Laelius de Amicitia*, written towards the end of his life, is significant not so much for the originality of its ideas as for the fact that it familiarized educated Romans for centuries to come with the idea that friendship should be at the centre of their serious concerns. The *De Amicitia* is a dramatic dialogue in the Socratic tradition, in which the historical figure of Laelius describes his friendship with the great Roman statesman Scipio Africanus. This enables

Cicero to treat many of the themes already discussed in Plato and Aristotle. Whether or not Cicero had read either directly, the stream of influence is clear. Cicero echoes Aristotle's definition of a friend as a 'second self' – an alter ego. Laelius (or Cicero) discusses how far true friendship is restricted to good men: he agrees that it is so, but is unwilling to make the definition of 'good' too narrow.[14] Other than wisdom, Laelius is made to say, there is no greater gift from the gods than friendship.[15] Friendship exists between two people, or at most a very small number.[16] The 'first law of friendship' is that a man does not ask his friend to do a dishonourable deed.[17] Cicero strongly criticizes the Epicurean idea that friendships are essentially self-interested, and the Stoic view that close friendships are to be shunned. Like the 'wisdom' books of the Old Testament, he discusses the risk to true friendship posed by prosperity, and wonders whether the wealth and influence of a powerful man cuts him off from real friends;[18] and he quotes the poet Ennius, 'Sure friends in unsure times are surely seen'.[19] One should be slow to think ill of a friend; and even if a friendship ends, a former friend still deserves a measure of respect.[20] The task of criticizing a friend, however difficult, is sometimes necessary.[21]

In his commentary on Cicero, J. G. F. Powell touches on the question we have already met in the case of David and Jonathan: how far were such friendships really political alliances, and how far do we misread an ancient text if we take it at what seems to us to be its face value? Powell points out that in the absence of political parties, a Roman politician advanced his career by means of a network of patronage and friendship. 'It appears to have been conventional', he says, 'for any form of political combination, or promise of support, to be accompanied by strong protestations of personal friendship, whether these were sincere or not.' Cicero's letters, though not the *De Amicitia*, bear this out. Powell insists that *amicitia* should not be used, as some historians have used it, simply as a technical term for such alliances: 'the claim of friendship could not work

4

St Augustine to St Aelred: A Developing Tradition

When in the year 375 the young Augustine, not yet a Christian, returned from the 'cauldron of illicit loves' at Carthage to become a teacher in his home town of Thagaste, he surrounded himself with a circle of friends. When one of them suddenly died, having accepted baptism on his deathbed, Augustine was both grief-stricken by the death and disturbed by the conversion, and it was to this circle that he naturally turned for comfort. And when in later years he recalled the experience in his *Confessions*, although he says that the love of his friends was then a substitute for loving God, there is no hint that he was wrong to have valued them as he did. The things that occupied his mind in the company of his friends, were, he says:

> To make conversation, to share a joke, to perform mutual acts of kindness, to read together well-written books, to share in trifling and in serious matters, to disagree though without animosity – just as a person debates with himself – and in the very rarity of disagreement to find the salt of normal harmony, to teach each other something or to learn from one another, to long with impatience for those absent, to welcome them with gladness on their arrival. These and other signs come from the heart of those who love and are loved and are expressed through the mouth, through the tongue, through the eyes, and a thousand gestures of delight,

acting as fuel to set our minds on fire and out of many to forge unity.[1]

Augustine, who was an authority on the works of Cicero, echoes a passage from the last pages of the *De Amicitia*, where Cicero speaks of the need 'to see into the other's heart, and lay your own open as well'.[2] Horace and Ovid are also evoked in his lament for his dead friend. Typically, Augustine is interested in his own reaction: was he, he wonders, attached more to his own grief than to the one for whom he grieved? Would he really have been willing to die for him – just as Orestes and Pylades were ready to die for one another?[3] Whatever answers he gives to his own questions, the terms in which Augustine ponders the heights and depths of friendship are that of any educated person of the time, pagan or Christian.

Augustine's friends continued to provide a chorus to the changing scenes of his life as he moved from being Manichee to Christian, teacher to priest to bishop. Between the time of his conversion and his baptism, he established a rural retreat for himself and his friends at Cassiacum, modelled on similar communities set up by wealthy Romans who wished to retire from the pressures of the world to read and discuss philosophy:

Among our group of friends we had had animated discussions of a project: talking with one another we expressed detestation for the storms and troubles of human life, and had almost decided on withdrawing from the crowds and living a life of contemplation . . . In sincere friendship nothing would be the private property of this or that individual, but out of the resources of all one treasury would be formed; the whole would belong to each, and everything would belong to everybody.[4]

Years later, as bishop of Hippo, he would form his priests into a resident celibate community, at once a monastery, a philosophical group and a circle of friends. He begins his treatise

'Concerning Faith of Things Not Seen' with the example of human friendship, from which, he says, we learn the nature of trust.[5] And later, when he wrote in the *City of God* that even human friendship is not proof against the tribulations of the world,[6] he was emphasizing the fragility of life, not diminishing the value of his friends.

The strains that circumstances impose upon relationships can be seen in another famous Christian friendship of about the same time, that of St Basil of Caesarea (*c.* 330–79) and St Gregory of Nazianzus (329–89).[7] Fellow students at Athens, they both became bishops in their native Cappadocia. In his panegyric after Basil's death, Gregory lauded their friendship: they were David and Jonathan, they were Orestes and Pylades. To later generations, Basil and Gregory themselves formed just such a legendary partnership;[8] but the reality was more strained. Episcopal office came between them. Gregory, the more classically minded, considered true friendship immutable; whereas Basil, it seemed to Gregory, put ecclesiastical affairs first, and Gregory felt neglected. He himself was of Athens, Gregory noted sadly; Basil was of Jerusalem. To the end of his days, Gregory mourned the loss, not only of his friend, but of his friendship.

It is in a monastic context that the idea of friendship is now taken up. Augustine's contemporary (and, on some theological subjects, antagonist) John Cassian discussed the nature of friendship in his *Conferences*. Cassian had been a monk in Bethlehem and later studied monastic developments in Egypt, but about 415 he established two monasteries near Marseilles and it was here for the rest of his life that he devoted himself to writing. The *Conferences* are imagined dialogues with the Fathers of Eastern monasticism; and in his 'First Conference with the Abbot Joseph', he describes three levels of friendship. The first arises when people are engaged in any sort of common enterprise or project – 'business or art or science or study' – or even crime. A higher level of friendship is to be found among those bound by ties of nature – 'those of the same tribe, wives and parents and brothers and children'.[9] Neither of these loves, says Cassian, which are common 'both to the good and the bad, and to beasts and serpents', can last for ever. There is, however, another kind of love, 'where the union is owing not to the favour of a recommendation, or some great kindness or gifts, or the reason of some bargain, or the necessities of nature, but simply to similarity of virtue'. This, he says, is 'the sure and indissoluble union of friendship, where the tie consists only in likeness in goodness'.[10]

Cassian adopts and alters Aristotle's threefold scheme of friendship; but he does more than distil the wisdom of the classics into his treatment of the Christian life. There is for Cassian only one serious Christian life, that of the monk: and therefore perfection of friendship can be found only between those who have embraced the monastic life. 'The first foundation of true friendship', Cassian goes on, 'consists in contempt for worldly substance and scorn for all things that we possess.'[11] Cassian does not quote the classical authors and is critical of those who study them, but we can see how much they inform his thought. Plato's discussion of whether friendship is possible only for the like-minded; Aristotle's insistence that only the virtuous can properly be friends; Cicero's observation that friendship is proved only when the distractions of prosperity are stripped away; above all the unspoken assumption that 'real' friendship is only found in an exclusively male context: all these reinforced the view that if there was to be such a thing as Christian friendship at all, then it was the monastery that would make it possible.

Mediaeval Christendom inherited the works of the Christian Fathers, as well as such works of the classical authors as happened to survive. (Plato survived; much of Aristotle was lost to the West for centuries but preserved in the Arab world; the study of Aristotle in the West was revived in the tenth century.) In his treatise *On Christian Doctrine,* St Augustine had already laid down that all the sciences known to the classical world had their place in a Christian scheme of knowledge. This was axiomatic to Western Christendom, and it opened the doors to a renewed study of the classical treatment of friendship. And so we come to the intellectual giant of the eleventh century, St Anselm.

Anselm was born in northern Italy in about the year 1033, and died in 1109. He became a monk at Bec in Normandy, attracted there by the charismatic personality of its prior, Lanfranc. He succeeded Lanfranc as prior, went on to become abbot, and then in 1093 succeeded Lanfranc again as Archbishop of Canterbury. He was a philosopher of the highest order. He was also a copious writer of letters, some four hundred of which have survived. As a monk and a teacher of monks, Anselm must have read Cassian and been familiar with his theory of friendship. He took Cassian's highest form of friendship and made it a central theme of his understanding of the monastic life, and it is through his letters that he gives expression to this.[12]

'Letters of friendship' were a convention of the time. If we think of Cassian's lowest class of friendship – the practical co-operation of those engaged in a common venture – then mediaeval Europe had developed a protocol of keeping such friendships in good repair by regular expressions of affection. So we find Lanfranc, Archbishop of Canterbury, writing to Thomas, Archbishop of York (with whom he did not get on very well) as his 'dearest brother and friend', and telling him that 'those who are joined in a sincere and Christian love suffer no division through bodily absence or geographical separation'. It sounds high-flown to us, and, knowing that the two prelates did not care that much for each other, somewhat insincere. The two men, however, were engaged on a common task that required co-operation; that, they both accepted, was a form of 'friendship', and so they submitted to the convention of regular expressions of affection as a necessary way of maintaining it.

Anselm, however, introduces a new and different note. His

'letters of friendship' are extravagant in the extreme and, as we would say, romantic. 'Enter into the chamber of your heart', he writes to Gundulf, who had been a fellow monk at Bec and then became Bishop of Rochester, 'and consider the impression of your own heart which you find there; from it you will recognize the love of your true friend.' To Gilbert Crispin, one of his former pupils at Bec whom Lanfranc had brought to England to be abbot of Westminster, he writes: 'If I were to describe the passion of our mutual love, I fear I should seem to those who do not know the truth to exaggerate. But you know how great is the affection we have experienced – eye to eye, kiss for kiss, embrace for embrace. I experience it all the more now when you, in whom I have had so much pleasure, are irretrievably separated from me.' Such letters, writes the great Anselmian scholar, Sir Richard Southern, 'suggest a world of emotional intensity nearer to that of twelfth-century romantic love than to traditional monastic friendship'.[13] But if these sound to us like love letters, we must bear in mind that Anselm addressed many of his friends in just such extravagant terms. They are letters that remind the recipients of the stern obligations of the monastic life on which they are all embarked; they are letters that Anselm himself considered fit for publication. He wanted others to read these extravagant expressions of friendship, and be drawn by them to the form of life which Anselm, like most of his contemporaries, regarded as the 'highest' – that of a monk. Anselm takes Cassian's last category of friendship, the union of souls in pursuit of a single aim, and provides it with a new language of its own.

Anselm not only provided the language of friendship with a new tone; he gave it a new theological purpose. The notion of a friend as another 'self', an alter ego, one for whom one might die, is, as we have seen, part of the classical rhetoric of friendship. St Augustine had asked himself whether he might have died for his friend. Anselm takes the idea of substitution, and makes of it not only a pillar of the monastic life but also the grounds of redemption. 'The joint soul created by fusion in a common monastic profession', writes Sir Richard Southern of the Anselmian doctrine of salvation, 'is not just a poetic image; it is a spiritual entity in the scale of being.'[14] 'The fusion of souls in friendship', he goes on, 'made possible the perfect substitution of one man for another, which on a cosmic scale dominated [Anselm's] doctrine of the Atonement. Indeed his theology and his doctrine of friendship alike presuppose the homogeneity of the human race and the ability of one man to stand in the place of another, united in will and profession.'[15] If the substitution of one self for another (Christ for fallen humanity) lies at the heart of the world's redemption, and if the substitution of one self for another (in the intensity of friendship) lies at the heart of the monastic life, then it follows that the monastic life, friendship and salvation are indivisible; and so it appears in Anselm's theology. He would have had all Christians enter the monastic life; he urged those who did not to live lives of like commitment, and if possible to take the monastic habit before death. The indivisibility of monastic life, friendship and salvation also explains the intensity of Anselm's language. As Southern puts it, 'The expressions which he used were not struck off in the heat of the moment in response to a passing mood, still less as the expression of a physical passion. Like everything else that he wrote, they were carefully considered, and their intensity was directly related to a theological plan.'[16] When Anselm writes of friendship, he is speaking the language of heaven.

In 1109, the year in which St Anselm died, St Aelred of Rievaulx was born at Hexham.[17] The first half of the twelfth century was the age of Peter Abelard, of the humanism of the new universities, of the intoxicating rediscovery of learning for learning's sake. In the spirit of St Augustine's doctrine that all arts and sciences find their home in a universe of Christian truth, the builders of Chartres placed Aristotle and Cicero among the figures on the west front of that cathedral, clustered about the Virgin and Child. But the twelfth century was also the age of St Bernard, Abelard's great adversary and the defender of orthodoxy; and the birth of a new stern Cistercian monasticism. St Aelred spans the age. In his youth he delighted in Cicero's *De Amicitia;* but later, as monk of the new Cistercian house at Rievaulx he wrote (at St Bernard's bidding) a book called *The Mirror of Charity*, in which he castigates those who read Virgil with the Gospels, Horace with the prophets, and Cicero with Paul. Later still, however, as abbot of Rievaulx, he wrote another book, in which he tried, as he says, to see whether he cannot give Cicero 'a foundation in the authority of scripture'. He begins by reflecting on the thoughtless friendships of his childhood, and acknowledges that it was Cicero who first made him think seriously about what he calls 'the laws of true friendship'. The resulting book, significantly called *On Spiritual Friendship* (*De Spiritali Amicitia*) is a bold re-working of the *De Amicitia*, in which the partners in dialogue are Aelred himself, and three fellow monks, Walter, Gratian and Ivo. Cicero's remark about there being only three or four pairs of friends celebrated in antiquity prompts the question whether friendship is too noble a thing to be attempted? 'But it is already a great thing to attempt great things,' Aelred replies. Did not the earliest Christians, he asks, who according to the Acts of the Apostles were of one heart and mind, and held all things in common, satisfy the classical requirements of friendship? Aelred thus constructs a bridge from the classical tradition of friendship to contemporary monasticism: for where, except in the purity of the Cistercian order, could the simplicity of the earliest Christians – and therefore the possibility of true friendship – be found?

Aelred goes on to distinguish friendship (*amicitia*) from charity (*caritas*, *agape*). We are commanded to show charity to all, even our enemies; friendship is possible only for those with whom we are united in soul. This prompts a further question: 'Shall I say of friendship what John, the friend of Jesus, says of charity: "God is friendship"?' 'That would be unusual, to be sure,' Aelred replies, 'nor does it have the sanction of the Scriptures. But still what is true of charity, I surely do not hesitate to grant to friendship, since he that abides in friendship, abides in God, and God abides in him.' Aelred is not setting up friendship as a virtue independent of love: 'the source and origin of friendship is love, for there can be love without friendship, but never friendship without love'. To feel the force of Aelred's words here we must return to *The Mirror of Charity*, where he dwells on the love between Christ and his 'friend' John:

> Some are joined to us more intimately and passionately than others in the lovely bond of spiritual friendship. And lest this sort of sacred love should seem improper to anyone, Jesus himself, in everything like us, patient and compassionate with us in every matter, transfigured it through the expression of his own love: for he allowed one, not all, to recline on his breast as a sign of his special love, so that the virgin head was supported in the flowers of the virgin breast, and the closer they were, the more copiously did the fragrant secrets of the heavenly marriage impart the sweet smell of spiritual charism to their virgin love. Although all the disciples were blessed with the sweetness of the greatest love of the most holy master, nonetheless he conceded as a privilege to one alone this symbol of a more intimate love, that he should be called 'the disciple whom Jesus loved'.[18]

'Friendship' is Aelred's most privileged class of relationship; but it is 'friendship' which can be described only in the language and imagery of married and erotic love.

Aelred's interlocutors in the *De Spiritali Amicitia* are still nervous that his ideal of friendship is too high for them (not surprisingly, in view of the passage just quoted); but Aelred humanizes the closing words of the dialogue. 'His lengthy concluding remarks on the practice of friendship,' says Fr Aelred Squire OP, 'which emphasize openness, cheerfulness, and equality, have the effect of relaxing the sense of effort, which his insistence on virtue has perhaps built up, and introduce the note of delicate, mutual courtesy which makes friendship a joy.'[19]

The monastic writers from John Cassian to St Aelred of Rievaulx retrieved the classical ideal of friendship for the Christian life; but they did so at a price. The classical ideal was closely interwoven with male circles of friends, philosophical conversation, the contemplative pursuit of goodness, retirement from the distractions of the world, and the notion that true friendship only appears when the snares of property and prosperity are stripped away. The monasteries fitted the pattern too well: only here, in poverty, seclusion and a life of prayer, could the classical ideal, adopted and adapted by theology, be realized.

Other Christians were, however, in the meantime discovering other ways of being friends.

5

Sworn Friends

From at least the third century, candidates for baptism were presented by sponsors. These were lay Christians who brought converts to the bishop, testified to their suitability for admission as catechumens, and accompanied the candidates during catechesis. At the baptism of infants, the sponsors made the profession of faith and the baptismal promises on their behalf. Pseudo-Dionysius (*c.* 500) speaks of the natural parents giving their child to another 'initiated' Christian, one who was 'a good teacher of children in divine things, that the child should live the rest of his life under him as under a divine father'.[1] This is one of the first references to sponsors as 'godparents', and points to a relationship between the baptized person and their sponsors which was expected to last beyond the moment of baptism.

The continuing relationship between godparent and godchild became increasingly important during the centuries that followed. St Augustine had already made a point of contrasting natural and spiritual generation (which ultimately goes back to John 3. 6: 'what is born of the flesh is flesh, and what is born of the Spirit is spirit'); but it had surprising consequences for church practice. If the relationship made at the font between sponsor and candidate was one of spiritual parenthood, it was increasingly felt necessary not to confuse it with natural kinship. In the sixth century, the emperor Justinian prohibited sponsors from marrying either their godchildren or their godchildren's natural parents. A principle of 'spiritual kinship' (*cognatio spiritualis*) was established, which was defined with increasing precision as time went on. An ecclesiastical council held in Prague in 1346, for instance, gave twenty cases in which spiritual kinship constituted an impediment to marriage: the ramifications of the 'Table of Kindred and Affinity' in the *Book of Common Prayer* are by comparison very straightforward. As John Bossy puts it in his *Christianity in the West 1400–1700*:

> In the late mediaeval centuries the history of the incorpora-
> tion of children into the community of Christians is a history
> of godparenthood. The characteristics of this much-appreci-
> ated institution were a tribute to the vigour and elegance of
> symbolic lay theology; they testified to a determination to
> make sure that on the other side of the waters of baptism the
> child would find itself received by a Christian kindred or gos-
> sip (god-sib) adequate to replace the natural kindred from
> which he had passed by the rites of regeneration, since flesh
> and blood could not inherit the kingdom of God.[2]

What every Christian received at the font was, in fact, a new set of friendships, spiritually constituted. Although there is no evidence that baptismal sponsorship in the early Church was classed as a 'friendship' – perhaps the language of spiritual 'parenthood' was too firmly established – it is clear that the spiritual kinship established at the font was one of a range of recognized and formal relationships available to the mediaeval Christian, which historians now sometimes classify as 'ritual friendships'. The easy intimacy of the relationship is shown by the way the word 'godsib' (spiritual relative) became 'gossip'. It was part of the cement of mediaeval society; one of the many ways in which mediaeval religion permeated every corner of 'secular' life. The guilds, and their close connection to the feast of Corpus Christi, the body and blood of Christ, functioned in the same way: both font and altar were socially as well as religiously cohesive.

The tradition of publicly acknowledged and formally committed friendship in mediaeval society, as well as some fascinating survivals of it into more recent times, is the subject of *The Friend* (2003), by the late Alan Bray. Bray explores, with many examples, the tradition of two men swearing lifelong friendship or 'brotherhood' to each other. The established relationship of godparent and godchild gave rise to the possibility that two men might also choose to be 'godbrothers'. Such sworn relationships (they could also be called 'wedded' – that is, pledged) were sanctioned by the Church; they were often made at the eucharist; and it was not uncommon for two such friends to be buried in the same grave. The symbolism of their funerary monuments can be strikingly reminiscent of married couples.

Take the case with which Bray begins his study: that of two distinguished English knights of the fourteenth century, Sir William Neville and Sir John Clanvowe. They were 'sworn brothers', and in 1391 they were on active service in Constantinople. Clanvowe died, and a few days later, overcome by grief, Neville followed him. The monks of Westminster Abbey in their chronicle placidly recorded their deaths, observing that the death of the one caused the other ('for whom his love was no less than for himself') 'such inconsolable sorrow that he never took food again and two days afterward breathed his last'. Not only did the monks of Westminster record their love; the friars of the Dominican church in Constantinople gave them burial. In 1913, their tomb was discovered, and they were found buried together. Their tombstone shows them both lying in full armour, but face to face and eye to eye. On their shields, each carries their own device impaled with the device of the other, which is the heraldic representation of a married couple. Their friendship evidently caused no difficulties either to the monks of Westminster or to the friars of Constantinople.[3]

Such 'sworn friendships' were not, as one might imagine, just for comrades-in-arms. The chapel of Merton College, Oxford displays the joint tomb of two of its fourteenth-century fellows, John Bloxham and John Whytton; as fellows, they were necessarily clerics and celibate. Their friendship began when Whytton entered the college in 1364, and Bloxham was already a fellow. It ended twenty years later, when Bloxham, by then warden of the college, died; and Whytton prepared a tomb for his friend in which he himself would also one day lie. On their memorial brass, which shows them side by side as so many of such brasses depict a married couple, they are dressed in clerical habit. It is not recorded that they had formally sworn friendship to each other; but evidently there was a profound and publicly acknowledged relationship between them. Their collegial, clerical and celibate status was clearly no barrier to this.

Both the Catholic Church of the West and the Orthodox Churches of the East had liturgical forms for the 'making of brothers' (*ordo ad faciendum fratrum; adelphopoiesis*); and Bray gives texts for these. One prayer, for instance, from a fourteenth-century manuscript from what appears to have been a Franciscan church in Croatia, includes the following words:

> Send your holy angel upon these your servants, N and N, that they may love each other, as your holy apostles Peter and Paul, and Andrew and James, and John and Thomas . . . not through the bonds of birth, but through faith and by the love of the Holy Spirit, that they may abide in the same love all the days of their life.[4]

The similarity of these words to the prayers of the marriage service hardly needs emphasizing. Bray points out, moreover, that surviving records of such occasions make it clear that they often took place at the church door, which was the traditional location for weddings. The church door strikingly symbolized both the public character of the commitment, and the fact that the relationship had a foot in both secular and spiritual society.

There are two further points to be made about the 'order for the making of brothers'. It includes antiphons for the introit and communion, and an epistle and gospel. The setting for the making of brothers was eucharistic. The communion antiphon is *Ecce quam bonum et quam iucundum habitare fratres in unum* ('Behold how good and pleasant it is when brothers dwell in unity').[5] The second thing to notice is the way the prayer quoted above beautifully inverts the customary order of the apostles, so that the natural brothers Peter and Andrew, and James and John, are not, for once, paired. The love invoked in this prayer is specifically not that of 'the bonds of birth' but rather that of the Spirit. *De spiritali amicitia* indeed.

The convention of sworn friendships survived the Reformation. Joint burials persisted, and from the seventeenth century evidence for the joint burials of women appears. Three hundred years after the monks of Westminster Abbey had unprotestingly recorded the sworn love of Sir William Neville and Sir John Clanvowe, their successors the dean and chapter allowed a monument to be erected in the Abbey to one Mary Kendall, the inscription of which records 'that close union and friendship in which she lived with the Lady Catherine Jones, and in testimony of which, she desired that even their ashes after death might not be divided, and therefore ordered herself here to be interred, where she knew that excellent lady designed one day to rest'.

Bray also uncovers evidence of women in the eighteenth and nineteenth centuries plighting their troth to each other, exchanging rings and sealing their friendship with a joint reception of holy communion. He traces out at length the friendship of Anne Lister and Ann Walker, from the evidence of Anne Lister's diary. In 1832, these women decided to settle as companions for life. 'We have agreed to solemnize our promise of mutual faith,' wrote Lister in her diary. On Easter Day 1834 they confirmed what they called their 'union' by receiving holy communion together at a church in York. A month earlier they had exchanged what they themselves described as wedding rings. Lister in her diary says of her friend, 'She is my wife in honour and in love and why not acknowledge her such openly and at once?'[6] Bray does not mention it, but we should remember that the mediaeval prohibition of marriage in Lent continued in practice well into the eighteenth century, which must have made Easter a popular time for weddings.[7] The association of Easter and marriage may have survived in folk memory as late as the

1830s. The other great association is that of Easter and the eucharist. That holy communion on Easter Sunday would have been one of the few celebrations of the eucharist in the course of the year in the pre-Victorian Church of England, but also one that would have been taken seriously by the whole parish. The occasion on which the two women chose to seal their 'union' was no private occasion, but one when they also sealed their fellowship with their Christian friends and neighbours. Bray traces out how the words which spontaneously found their way into Anne Lister's diary – 'union', 'faith', 'wed' – are the terms not only of marriage but also of the tradition of sworn friendship going back five hundred years. And the instinct that led the two women to solemnize their union at the eucharist was one that the 'godbrothers' who knelt at the altar in that Franciscan church in Croatia and elsewhere would have understood.

The similarities between the making friends and the ceremonies of marriage are all the greater when we consider the variety of marriage custom that survived in England until the 1753 Act of Parliament 'For the Better Preventing of Clandestine Marriages'. This Act required that every marriage (with the exception of those of Jews and Quakers) should take place in an Anglican church before a clergyman, after the calling of banns (or a licence that dispensed with banns), followed by an entry in the parish marriage register. The effect of it was to sweep away the traditional variety of marriage custom that had survived from mediaeval times. Marriage 'at the church door' was forbidden. So was the custom of a couple simply reading the marriage service to each other and exchanging a ring; or of exchanging vows and rings in a garden; or breaking a gold piece; or drawing up a wedding contract and then receiving holy communion. As Bray shows, all of these can be documented from diocesan consistory court records in the eighteenth century. In other words, they were all forms of marriage which the Church of England accepted and recorded as such. And they were deeply traditional: as Bray says, 'These are forms that would have been as readily intelligible in the fifteenth century –

if not in the eleventh century – as in the eighteenth.'[8] Seventy years after the passing of the Act – not long in terms of the persistence of folk memory – Anne Lister and Ann Walker 'sealed their union' in a manner that, had the Act not intervened, would have been recognized as one age-old way of marrying. Clearly they thought of it in that light.

So, were Anne Lister and Ann Walker 'married'? Or those two knights, Sir William Neville and Sir John Clanvowe; or those two clerical fellows of Merton College, John Bloxham and John Whytton? In what sense are we talking here of homosexual relationships, and did those who knew of the friendships of these pairs of friends take it for granted that they were sexual? We can widen the question: when Christian writers spoke rhapsodically of the 'friendship' of two people of the same sex, did they have a homosexual relationship in mind? Remember the words that St Anselm wrote to Abbot Gilbert Crispin: 'You know how great is the affection we have experienced – eye to eye, kiss for kiss, embrace for embrace. I experience it all the more now when you, in whom I have had so much pleasure, are irretrievably separated from me.' Is this the language of homosexuality?

It is both predictable and proper that during the past quarter-century historians have been searching the past for evidence of homosexual relationships. In the 1980s the American historian John Boswell produced evidence (quite startling at the time) of what he called 'same-sex unions'. On the basis of his evidence he argued that the Church had regularly sanctioned what today we would understand as homosexual relationships. Much of his material is valuable, and is not dissimilar to that which is covered by Alan Bray. His arguments, however, have been subjected to some very severe scholarly criticism, not least by the great Anselmian scholar, Sir Richard Southern, in the book on Anselm to which we referred in the last chapter:

Boswell invariably speaks of homosexuality as a well-recognized physiological or psychological state, which finds its normal expression in a wide range of 'homosexual activities', extending indiscriminately, as far as I can judge, from kissing to sodomy; and he deals with the subject as if an attitude similar to this existed in the eleventh century.[9]

Southern goes on to show that kissing, embracing or the writing of letters of ardent and passionate love between two men did not convey the meanings in the eleventh century that they would do for us. The kiss, for instance, was an important ceremony in both religious and secular life, and an act of the utmost symbolic significance: King Henry II refused the kiss of peace to Thomas Becket, which meant their quarrel must continue to its catastrophic end; St Hugh, Bishop of Lincoln, resolved a quarrel with King Richard I by tugging at his cloak until the king at last agreed to kiss him. Southern dismisses Boswell's claim that the letters of St Anselm betray a latent, or not so latent, homosexuality; indeed, he points out that Anselm, true to his time, reprobated 'sodomy' in the strongest terms. That in itself, of course, might not be convincing, for it is human nature to denounce in others what one is ashamed of in oneself. But Anselm does not stand on his own: his references to kissing and embracing place him firmly in the ordinary mediaeval world. *Those* things, for him, had nothing to do with 'sodomy' at all. Anselm tells us what, in his view, *does* encourage 'sodomy': it is long hair in men, and effeminate clothing. This illustrates very clearly how lines are simply being drawn in different places from where we would draw them today.

The same is true of the bed. For us, the shared bed is the very symbol of a sexual relationship, because for us a bed (and a bedroom) is a place of privacy. 'Sleeping together' is a euphemism for sexual intercourse. But beds and bedchambers could not carry the same weight of symbolic overtone for a culture in which sleeping arrangements were rarely private, whether in the king's palace or the peasant's cottage: which is why we find all those ancient titles of royal functionaries like the clerk of the closet and the gentleman of the bedchamber so quaint, while at the time they simply reflected life as lived.

Bray interestingly traces the gradual invasion of domestic life, throughout the eighteenth century, by symbols and habits of privacy; it marks, for him, the transition from a 'traditional' to a 'civil' society. Foreigners began to notice that Englishmen shook hands rather than kissed. That this first took place in England, leaving continental Europe practising the courtesies of a more traditional age, gave the English a store of humour (or indignation) at the expense of foreigners, which is not yet wholly exhausted. By 1749, an Englishman could be offended at the sight of two men kissing each other in public: as Bray says, 'He seems to have been unaware that it had ever been thought otherwise.'[10]

Southern's criticisms of Boswell (which Boswell himself dismissed in a footnote as 'cranky'[11]) are echoed by Bray. He criticizes Boswell for taking it for granted that what was being effected in the rites of 'making brothers' was a kind of homosexual marriage, with the expectation of homosexual intercourse and the consequent exclusion of the possibility of heterosexual marriage. This, says Bray,

> ... glosses over the historical disparity that, in the past, marriage has been one, as it is not in modern society, among several forms of what one might call voluntary kinship: kinship created not by blood but by ritual or a promise. The claim that the relationships blessed by this rite were sexual and akin to marriage, *and* the claim that they were not, both involve an unsettling degree of anachronism.[12]

In other words, if we approach the study of sworn friendships in the past with the question I posed above, 'Were they married?', comparing and contrasting them to marriage as we know it today, then we shall misread them. Friendship and marriage – and spiritual kinships such as those of godparent and godchild – all belonged to a very rich Christian society in which people could enter into a variety of recognized relationships with one another. 'Friendship', as we have seen, was a virtue widely recognized and deeply rooted in that society, celebrated by Christian and classical authors alike; it was sufficiently distinct to hold its own against relationships derived from sex and birth. The assumption that 'friendship' either means sex, or else must be demoted (as we do) to 'just friendship' is a very modern (and singularly blinkered) point of view.

This is not the same as saying that no 'sworn' or 'wedded' friendship was ever sexual. How could that be proved or disproved – especially at periods when 'sodomy' was a serious (or even capital) offence? If two 'sworn brothers' had sex together, they would be careful to keep the fact secret: their lives might depend on it. The evidence is necessarily elusive to the point of invisibility. All that we might take to be evidence today – the love letter, the embrace, the kiss, the solemnly sealed union, the exchanged ring, the shared bed and the shared grave – turns out to be part of the ordinary shared life of mediaeval society. If these things were generally recognized as a mere cloak for what the mediaeval Church called 'sodomy', then the mediaeval Church would not have so actively sanctioned the institution of sworn friendship.

But the question is not just one of the availability of evidence. What, after all, would count in an earlier culture as evidence of what today we would regard as a homosexual or a gay relationship? We must be mindful of Southern's warning against thinking of 'homosexuality' as 'a well-recognized physiological or psychological state, which finds its normal expression in a wide range of "homosexual activities"' – as well-recognized in any earlier century as our own. Southern and Bray on the one hand, and Boswell on the other, represent different positions on a spectrum of opinion described by David Greenberg, in his massive work *The Construction of Homosexuality* (1988), as that of 'constructivists' and 'essentialists'. The constructivist end of the spectrum emphasizes the variability of sexual behaviour from one culture to another, and the variability of the symbolism that that behaviour carries for that particular culture.

The essentialist end of the spectrum looks for the continuities of both behaviour and meaning from one culture to another. Boswell, for instance, representing an essentialist point of view, assumes that what we would take to be evidence today of a homosexual relationship can be fairly straightforwardly transferred to an earlier society as evidence for a comparable kind of relationship then. A constructivist approach, such as that of Southern or Bray, is more sensitive to the differences between cultures, both in behaviour and symbolism. Greenberg (as the title of his book suggests) also represents a constructivist point of view: as he says, 'Sexual practices and the ways they are socially organized vary greatly from one society to another and ... the conceptual categories through which people think about sex are also variable.'[13] This, however, is not the same as saying that types of behaviour are simply invented by society. That some mediaeval men had sex together is perfectly plain, or it would not have been forbidden. That some mediaeval men, who longed for a persistent sexual relationship with a male partner, found the framework for doing so within the conventions of 'sworn friendship' seems likely. But to suggest that that is all that sworn friendship meant, or that its formal similarity to the conventions of marriage permit us to blur the boundary between the two, does not do justice to the ways traditional Christian society celebrated the gift of friendship.

Furthermore, the idea that the tradition of 'sworn friendship' was 'nothing but' the framework for homosexual relationships in disguise does not take account of formal friendships between men and women; to that we turn next.

6

Men and Women

Beloved, I can write to you only very hurriedly; yet I had to try to write to you something, however brief, in the hope of giving you if I can a little joy. You are so deeply engraven on my heart that the more I realize how truly you love me from the depths of my soul, the more incapable I am of forgetting you and the more constantly you are in my thoughts; for your love moves me deeply and makes my love for you burn more strongly.[1]

These lines occur in a letter written by the second Master of the Order of Preachers and successor of St Dominic, Jordan of Saxony, in the spring of 1228, to Diana d'Andalo. Contemporaries remembered Diana as beautiful, charming and intelligent; she became one of the first Dominican sisters, and the lifelong friend of Jordan. His letters to her, written between 1222 and 1236, of which fifty have survived, show that the language of ardent affection, which we have already encountered in St Anselm, both persisted and readily transferred itself to the friendship of a man and a woman. Of course, their shared vocation to chastity was not in doubt. Nonetheless, the intimate tone of Jordan's letters is remarkable, and evidently caused no embarrassment to the brothers of the order who carefully assembled them after his death. Jordan and Diana met for the last time in 1233. She died three years later, and in the spring of 1237 Jordan was lost at sea while returning from the Holy Land.

A new theological foundation for friendship was laid by St Thomas Aquinas, who joined the Order of Preachers about seven years after Jordan's death. His massive philosophical achievement was based upon a synthesis of the Scriptures and early Christian Fathers with the work of Aristotle. His treatment of personal relationships takes both 'charity' (*agape, caritas*) and 'friendship' (*philia, amicitia)* as given categories; the one, on the authority of the New Testament, and the other, on the authority of Aristotle. In his *Summa Theologiae* he teases out the relationship between them. The Pauline concept of *agape* implies something universal in scope, embracing the sinful as well as the virtuous. Aristotle, on the other hand, limited perfect friendship to the virtuous only, on the grounds that all friendship required some shared interests, and those of the vicious could not sustain a perfect friendship. On the face of it, then, *agape* and *philia* are different things. Aquinas, however, argues that in the case of *agape*, it is God who provides the common ground by seeking to share his happiness with us; God therefore raises *agape* to the status of *philia*.[2] Elsewhere, he says that 'human justice, which consists in the observance of law, is consummated in one precept of charity; the fullness of this law is friendship'.[3]

St Thomas's inclusion of friendship within the scheme of Christian theology has implications for his doctrine of marriage. Marriage, too, he says, is a form of friendship:

> The form of matrimony is an inseparable union of souls in which husband and wife are pledged in an unbreakable bond of mutual love, and the purpose is the birth and training of children. Obviously, the birth of children is started through sexual intercourse, but their training is carried through by other functions of the husband and wife as when they help each other to bring up the children.[4]

The doctrine of 'an inseparable union of souls' takes us straight back to what Aristotle says in Book 9 of the *Nicomachean Ethics* about the indissolubility of true friendship and the friend as a 'second self'. Aristotle himself spoke of marriage as a kind of friendship, though one that suffered from the radical inequality of husband and wife. St Thomas builds on this, and puts marriage into all three of Aristotle's categories of friendship: the useful, the pleasurable and the virtuous:

> Married friendship is useful, delightful, and honourable. It serves to provide for domestic life. It brings the delights of sex, and the physical pleasure that animals have. And if husband and wife are fair to one another, their friendship is expressed in virtue proper to them, rendering it mutually agreeable.[5]

St Thomas's doctrine that friendship is a more fundamental category than marriage opens the way to a positive evaluation of the friendship between men and women. For if friendship is the fundamental category, then non-marital friendships between men and women are not in some way failed or half-hearted approximations to marriage; they are relationships that stand in their own right and have their own integrity.

This was emphatically insisted upon by St Francis de Sales (1567–1622), the Catholic Bishop of Geneva, and author of the widely influential *Introduction to the Devout Life*. This book, one of the first manuals of spirituality specifically designed for those living in a secular environment, arose out of the spiritual direction he gave to his cousin by marriage, Mme de Charmoisy. The book is addressed to her throughout under the name of 'Philothea'. A more famous friendship also lies behind the book. St Jane Frances de Chantal was an aristocratic widow, who took a vow of chastity and placed herself under St Francis's direction. Together they founded the Visitandines, a contemplative order for women.

St Francis de Sales devotes four chapters of the *Introduction* to friendship. 'Love everyone with a full and charitable love,' he tells Philothea, echoing a now familiar refrain of the Aritotelian-Augustinian-Thomist tradition, 'but have no friendship at all except with those who can have fellowship with you in the things of virtue.'[6] 'Virtuous' friendships, says St Francis, can be enjoyed with family, relatives, benefactors, neighbours and others; there is no need to renounce any of them; but there is room for more selective friendships too. Are these a problem? 'Many will say perhaps that we ought not to have any kind of particular affection and friendship, inasmuch as it occupies the heart, distracts the spirit, and produces jealousy.'[7] While he concedes that there may be a danger in particular friendships in the context of a monastery, such considerations do not apply to those who are in 'the world'; 'for by means of this they encourage one another, they help one another, they stir up one another to good works'.[8] 'Sacred friendship' has a freedom and candour about it: it 'has a language which is simple and frank'; it 'has only simple and modest eyes, free and frank caresses'; it 'has its eyes wide open and does not hide itself'.[9]

Men and women may, of course, deceive themselves that their friendships are innocent when they are not. St Francis is clear about the need for both self-discipline and self-knowledge. When he talks about friendships that have turned (as he would say) 'carnal' it is clear that he means friendship between the sexes; but he does not for that reason reject them. They could have remained innocent and 'sacred'. As he boldly points out, particular friendships – and friendships between the sexes – are rooted in the life and example of the Lord:

We could not deny that our Lord loved with a gentler and more special friendship St John, Lazarus, Martha, Magdalen, for the Scripture bears witness to it . . . St Gregory Nazianzen boasts a hundred times of the unique friendship he enjoyed with the great St Basil . . . St Augustine bears witness that St Ambrose had a unique love for St Monica, because of the rare virtues which he saw in her; and that she had a mutual affection for him as an angel of God.[10]

There is a strong echo of St Aelred of Rievaulx here, but the stress upon friendship across the sexes is typically that of St Francis de Sales.

Puritanism was less hospitable to the idea that friendship might exist both between the sexes and outside marriage. At once more positive about sex, more pragmatic about marriage (and divorce), and more suspicious of celibacy, than the heirs of the pre-Reformation tradition, the Puritans sought to make of marriage the only proper context for male–female friendship. The works of St Francis de Sales, on the other hand, enjoyed a remarkable popularity among those seventeenth-century Anglicans who were not averse to reading Roman Catholic books. The *Introduction* was one of the volumes that the Ferrar family bound specially for their collection at Little Gidding. De Sales' work was also known to Jeremy Taylor, whose own 'Discourse on the Nature Offices and Measures of Friendship' dealt specifically with friendships between the sexes, and was addressed to his lifelong friend the poet Katharine Philips.[11] Another devout Anglican who read de Sales was the friend of Taylor and Philips, John Evelyn, whose 'spiritual friendship' with Margaret Godolphin is a remarkable story.

John Evelyn (1620–1706) is best known as a diarist, though not as famous as his contemporary Pepys. He was throughout his life both a Royalist and a devout Anglican, a man of wide interests who played a part in the foundation of the Royal Society. In the troubled years of the Civil War, at the Paris home of a friend, Sir Richard Browne, he met and married Browne's young daughter Mary, who bore him children and outlived his long life by three years. In 1669 he met the young Margaret Blagge, a member of the Queen Mother's household. Witty and attractive, Margaret could hold her own at court; and she combined this, not wholly exceptionally, with a very serious Anglican piety. In 1675 she married a fellow courtier Sidney Godolphin and died in childbirth in 1678.

From 1665 until her death, she and Evelyn were friends. The intellectual climate of the time was hospitable to Platonist ideas, and 'friendship' naturally figured as a matter of discussion and practical experience in the circles in which Evelyn moved. The scientist Robert Boyle introduced the phrase 'Seraphick Love', following Castiglione's exposition of platonic love in the *Book of the Courtier*. 'Nuptial love maketh mankind,' wrote Francis Bacon in his essay 'On Friendship', 'friendly love perfecteth it.' In his 'Discourse', Jeremy Taylor admitted that while marriage ought to be 'the queen of friendships' in practice a spouse might be 'not so proper for all relations of friendship'. In Clarendon's essay 'On Friendship', he suggested that friendship was 'more a Sacrament' than marriage.

The climate of 'platonic' or 'seraphick' love presupposed a culture in which sex was regarded as ignoble (however necessary or irresistible). In the *Religio Medici*, that genial and humane doctor, Sir Thomas Browne, wrote:

> I could be content that we might procreate like trees, without conjunction, or that there were any way to perpetuate the world without this trivial and vulgar way of union: it is the foolishest act a wise man commits in all his life; nor is there anything that will more deject his cool'd imagination, when he shall consider what an odd and unworthy piece of folly he hath committed.[12]

Browne is giving voice to the conventional platonism of the day. Interestingly, the bishop is rather more positive about sex than the doctor. In his 'Rules for Married Persons', Jeremy Taylor defines four functions of sex: a 'desire for children', to 'avoid fornication', to 'lighten and ease the cares and sadnesses of household affairs', and to 'endear each other'. Sexual desire, he says, should never be separated from these ends, but 'always be joined with all *or one*' of them; which is quite a liberal point of view. It is hedged about, however, with warnings against immoderate sensuality; the sexual act should be done, the bishop gravely says, 'without violent transporting desires'.[13] In a culture which found it hard to say anything both serious and affirmative about the appetites of the body, and in which, as Harris says, 'prescription and patriarchal authority still prevailed' in marriage, it was natural to speak of 'platonic' love as essentially superior to all other relationships. Harris again: 'In any society of rigidly prescribed and unequal social roles, friendship was likely to be highly valued for the freedoms and emotional satisfactions it offered.'[14]

In his friendship with Margaret Godolphin, John Evelyn explored the potential of such ideas. His love for her was ardent, and in 1672 he persuaded her to agree a formal pact of friendship. They signed a paper which Evelyn prepared, embellished with the sketch of an altar upon which a heart is pointed upwards to heaven. They met each Tuesday for conversation, Evelyn acting as something of a spiritual director. When she was abroad, he renewed their 'sacrament of perpetual friendship' (as he called it) by reciting the office of All Saints each Tuesday, the collect of which speaks of the 'elect' as 'knit together in one communion and fellowship'. John Evelyn and Margaret Godolphin were far from unique in their 'seraphick' love; but it was almost uniquely recorded for posterity.

Evelyn privately wrote a 'Life' of Margaret after her death; it was first published in 1847, and became a bestseller. In the twentieth century the relationship of Evelyn and Godolphin was subjected to critical study of a more post-Freudian temper; the story of a married man forming a 'spiritual' friendship with an attractive girl half his age was bound to come in for unsympathetic scrutiny.[15] In 2003 Frances Harris published a major new study of the relationship, *Transformations of Love,* and this has moved the debate beyond the predictable reactions of both nineteenth and twentieth centuries and set it for the first time in the context of the contemporary discussions of love and friendship. As Harris says, 'passionate friendships between men and women who were unconnected by marriage or kinship, centred in shared religious practice, were and are a feature of many sects and periods of Christianity'.[16] She goes on:

> There is no need for us to be unduly knowing or condescending about these. De Sales wrote quite frankly of 'the similarity that exists between our spiritual emotions and our

physical passions'. The aspect of sublimated sexuality was well understood, and indeed valued, by the participants, who never discounted the unruly and subversive nature of sexual passion. We may now take it for granted that passionate sexual love demands physical expression, whatever the consequences if it should arise outside accepted social norms or in competition with other claims, but we may need reminding that this has not always been seen as the only or the best solution. It is clear enough ... that at one level Evelyn was 'in love' with Margaret Blagge and knew that he was. The crucial issue was how he dealt with it.[17]

Harris traces out the story of the relationship so far as it can be reconstructed from Evelyn's substantial surviving archive. Clearly, Margaret was a spirited person who made her own decisions (especially about her own marriage) and was far from being under Evelyn's control, despite all his plans for her spiritual welfare. The two other main characters in the drama, Mary Evelyn and Sidney Godolphin, remain partly but not wholly in the background; we have less opportunity to see at close hand what the 'holy friendship' of their respective spouses meant to them. Taylor was firmly of the view, despite his acknowledgement of the limitation of marriage, that husbands and wives 'must have an affection greater to each other than they have to any person in the world, but no greater than they have to God.'[18] Whether this precept really governed the relationship of John Evelyn and Mary Godolphin is impossible to say. That the 'friendship' was not a physical sexual relationship in disguise seems clear enough; but the point at which a friendship begins to trespass emotionally on the fidelity of marriage is harder to determine. The interest of the story for us is the way in which the tradition of 'spiritual friendship' is exemplified in a particularly well-documented episode.

The only drawback of Harris's excellent study is that it appeared at the same time as Alan Bray's *The Friend*; neither book could incorporate the evidence and insights of the other, though together they illuminate the persistence of the tradition of formal friendships. In particular, the sacramental 'pact' of friendship, however quaint or questionable it may seem to us for two married people to engage upon, clearly stands in that long convention of formalized friendships which Bray has documented.

Our study so far has suggested that the clear distinctions between *agape*, *philia* and *eros*, so familiar to readers of C. S. Lewis's, *The Four Loves*, cannot be maintained so sharply. St Thomas Aquinas, following Aristotle, classified married love as a sort of friendship, and certainly the language of friendship is present in the rites of marriage, from the 'mutual society, help and comfort' of *The Book of Common Prayer*, to the 'strength, companionship and comfort' of *Common Worship*. But if the Puritans tried to confine friendship between men and women within the bounds of marriage, Christian experience told otherwise. Men made friends with men, and women with women, and women with men. The friendships of men and women did not have to be marriages, and the more catholic part of the Christian tradition encouraged a high and sacramental view of such relationships. If in the Christian tradition there is this degree of overlapping ground between married love and the love of friends, then what light does this shed upon the Church's current preoccupation with the union (married or otherwise) of homosexual people?

7

Friendship and Homosexuality

In Chapter 5 we considered the difficulty of deciding what would count as evidence of a 'homosexual relationship' in the past. John Boswell, and the 'essentialist' position he represented, looked for continuities of behaviour between past ages and our own. The 'constructivist' position of David Greenberg and others, on the other hand, is more impressed by the discontinuities of behaviour between one culture and another, the variety of ways in which different sorts of sexual behaviour are publicly signalled, and the diversity of meanings that those sorts of behaviour can carry in different societies. As Greenberg says, few non-Western societies would make any of the assumptions now widely accepted in Western culture about what constitutes a 'homosexual relationship'. Few non-Western societies, for instance, would accept an equal status for male–male and female–female relationships; and many would count differences of age and social status as critically important.

This is important when we come to consider the Church's long-standing antipathy to homosexual acts. For that antipathy is rooted in certain authoritative prohibitions which are unavoidably specific to the cultures in which they were made. If homosexual acts are condemned in some parts of the biblical tradition, we still have to ask exactly what was being condemned, and why. What did those acts symbolize and signify in that society? How transferable are those meanings, and therefore those prohibitions, to another culture?

The Church's antipathy to homosexual acts is principally rooted in two parts of the biblical tradition: the 'holiness code' of Leviticus, and the letters of St Paul. That does not make it less significant, but it does move the debate away from some other passages that have sometimes been considered relevant. The story of Sodom in Genesis 19, for instance, which gave the Church its term 'sodomy', apparently concerns a violent homosexual gang-rape and an appalling abuse of the obligations of hospitality to strangers: there are too many different offences involved in the story for the homosexual aspect to be singled out as such. Again, the prohibition of male and female cult prostitutes in Deuteronomy 23 is at once too general (the prostitution of both sexes is equally condemned) and too restricted (to the worship of the Temple) to serve as a ground for condemning just homosexual acts in society at large. The fact is that few ancient Near Eastern societies, if any, condemned homosexual activity; and Greenberg provides a wealth of evidence for this.[1] In the light of this evidence, Greenberg concludes that until Leviticus, there is no evidence that 'the Hebrews viewed homosexuality any differently from the way other peoples of the ancient Near East viewed it'.[2]

The Book of Leviticus reflects the reforms of the time of the building of the second Temple in 517 BC. Following the catastrophic loss of the first Temple, and the exile of Israel to Babylon, the Levitical reformers set out a programme of 'holiness' designed symbolically to separate the people of God ever more decisively from the peoples of the surrounding cultures. The 'holiness' that was once concentrated in the Temple was to be realized within Israel as a whole. Much of this 'holiness' was to do with concepts of bodily purity and pollution. Sexual intercourse between two men was part of a whole programme of sexual prohibitions designed to safeguard the purity and holiness of the people of God.[3] On the other hand, there was no ban on sexual acts between two women.

A pronounced inequality between men and women runs through most of the Old Testament. The act of sexual penetration (and the Old Testament seems to know nothing of any other sexual activity) was symbolically expressive of 'taking possession', for 'taking possession' is what men did to women. A man was not prohibited from penetrating an unmarried woman, for that was tantamount to 'taking possession' of her, which he was free to do. But he might not penetrate a married woman, nor might a married woman consent to such an act, for that would be to violate the rights of possession of the woman's husband. For two men to engage in a penetrative sexual act with each other (or for a man or a woman to engage in a sexual act with a beast) was similarly to alter the hierarchy both of sex and of society. And in a society such as that reflected in Leviticus, in which there was a profound anxiety about offending God all over again and risking the loss of land and Temple a second time, a disturbance of the sexual ordering of society became a matter of the utmost gravity.[4]

If we ask the further question why such a society constructed itself upon a principle of male dominance, the answer is likely to be many-stranded; but at least part of it must lie in the pressure upon ancient societies simply to survive. The replenishment of the species for labour on the land and combat in the field was a priority, not least for a tribe that acknowledged the call of God to be his chosen race. Describing the very much more developed condition of the second-century Roman Empire, Peter Brown tells us:

> Citizens of the Roman Empire at its height were born into the world with an average life expectancy of less than twenty-five years. Death fell savagely on the young. Those who survived childhood remained at risk. Only four out of every hundred men, and fewer women, lived beyond the age of fifty. It was a population 'grazed thin by death'.[5]

Israel half a millennium earlier was in an even more precarious situation. It was of paramount importance that the possibilities of procreation were maximized. Men were brought up to long for a vast and healthy progeny; in a culture that had no positive expectation of the afterlife (and that goes for almost all the Old Testament), to live on in one's children and grandchildren was a desirable kind of immortality. Polygamy, and rules requiring widows to marry their brothers-in-law, increased the chances of it. Women were taught to fear the stigma of being barren, as we can see in so many Old Testament stories. Brown tells us that for the population of the Roman Empire to remain static, each woman needed to give birth to at least five children. He goes on to speak of the 'huge pain that any underdeveloped society places on the bodies of its fertile women'.[6]

Greenberg's evidence shows that the pressure to survive did not of itself create a climate hostile to homosexual activity. He does, however, draw attention to the rise in late antiquity of 'an asceticism that was hostile to all forms of sexual pleasure'. He argues that this developed within new dualistic forms of religion that 'opposed good and evil, spirit and flesh, male and female, which were largely unknown to pagan polytheism'. Character-istic of this was Zoroastrianism, which profoundly influenced the growth of a dualistic theology in post-exilic Israel, and had a stern aversion to homosexual activity.[7] The growth of this dualism Greenberg in turn attributes to a range of causes, including the rise of urban societies in which the old symbiosis of agriculture, fertility and religion no longer held good; and a series of catastrophic wars and conquests that engulfed Mediterranean society, creating a climate of anxiety and a ten-dency to withdraw from 'the world'.[8] It is in this context that sexuality comes to be seen as suspect, except for the serious business of procreation. Greenberg sees Leviticus as showing early symptoms of this rise of anxiety and asceticism.

If there were powerful reasons for the prohibition of homo-sexual acts in Leviticus, those reasons became no less cogent as the history of Israel unfolded. The exilic and inter-testamental books are increasingly strident on the subject of marriage with foreigners. As the land was lost or overrun, so the distinctive-ness of the people became ever more and more urgent. It was unthinkable that there should have been any relaxation of the sexual laws which were now firmly fixed in the sacred law.

It was into this world that Jesus was born. As we know, Jesus was steeped in the Scriptures of his ancestors. As we also know, he freely reinterpreted some of them to an astonishing extent. But Jesus was not simply a moral teacher; indeed, he was hardly a moral teacher at all, in the sense of offering systematic ethical teaching for its own sake. Jesus was burdened with the kingdom of God and the need, in a very short space of time, to convince his fellow Israelites (and especially their religious leaders) that they were radically mistaking the divine purpose if they supposed that God was about to lead them into battle against the Romans and restore the kingdom of David by force of arms. The true Israel, he taught, was not defined by blood or by land or by their obedience to the law of Moses. This meant some wholesale jettisoning of sacred traditions: the sabbath was made for humankind, for instance, not humankind for the sabbath.

All this left his followers with some profoundly unanswered questions (Jesus was good at not answering the questions people wanted him to answer). The most searching one to engage the Church early on was to do with the admission of Gentiles, and whether they were bound by the law of Moses or not. In particular, must they be circumcised as Jews before they could be baptized as Christians? The verdict of the apostolic council at Jerusalem, not universally accepted, but enthusiastically promoted by the convert Paul of Tarsus, was that Gentiles were largely free of the law of the Old Testament. Not, of course, said St Paul, that Gentile Christians were free of God's moral law written on every human heart, but in the main they were free of the prescriptions of the law of Moses. According to the Epistle to the Ephesians Christ 'has abolished the law with its commandments and ordinances, so that he might create in himself one new humanity in place of two'.[9] So where did Paul draw the line between the moral law which God has written on the human heart and the transient law of Moses which Christ had set aside? And into which category did the Levitical prohibition of homosexual acts (about which Jesus is not recorded as having said anything) fall?

Within certain strict boundaries, Roman society tolerated homosexual acts; but only on the part of its male citizens. That is not to say that it recognized a condition, disposition or orientation called 'homosexuality', for which it had no word. There was no acknowledgement in Roman society, any more than in any other part of the ancient world, that some people might just be heterosexual and others homosexual. The accepted Roman view was that in some contexts a man might engage in homosexual acts, according to his taste or pleasure, without blame. The freedom to take sexual pleasure with one's wife or concubine, with one's slaves of either sex, or with an adolescent boy of one's choice, was a sign of freedom and complete masculine humanity. The only fully formed human beings in Roman culture, in fact, were free men. Children, adolescents, women and slaves all fell short of that fully formed male humanity.[10] That freedom was qualified by two things. The first was the duty to replenish the city with Roman boys (the Emperor Augustus passed laws to ensure that everyone did their bit). The second qualification was to do with the sexual role adopted by the free man. To be a passive partner in sex was to compromise one's masculine dignity. It was the job of the free man to penetrate and not to be penetrated: that was a critical moral distinction for the Romans. Penetration proclaimed ownership; and a man who allowed himself to be buggered was relinquishing his mastery, allowing himself to become a woman, a slave, an adolescent. That was deeply shameful.[11]

When Paul looked at pagan Roman culture, he saw a set of sexual conventions that symbolized mastery and subordination, dominance and submission. At the heart of it was a vast idolatry that subverted the purposes of the Creator and, as he wrote in the Epistle to the Romans, could lead only to a 'darkening of the mind'. Once that happened then the Creator abandoned people to their own devices. Deprived of all moral bearings, they could not but drift into acts of shameless debauchery, the disgrace of which was its own punishment. Characteristic of that morass, says Paul, is the exchange on the part of both women and men of natural sexual relations for unnatural:

> For this reason God gave them up to degrading passions. Their women exchanged natural intercourse for unnatural, and in the same way also the men, giving up natural intercourse with women, were consumed with passion for one another. Men committed shameless acts with men and received in their own persons the due penalty for their error.[12]

In 1 Corinthians, Paul lists those people whose 'wrong-doing' will disinherit them from the kingdom of God. Along with fornicators, adulterers, idolaters, thieves and drunkards, are *malakoi* and *arsenokoitoi*.[13] Although some have maintained that St Paul's use of these terms is unclear, the distinction between the two terms is plain enough. The *malakoi* are the 'soft men' – the Greek word for those who take the passive role in a sexual act; the *arsenokoitoi* are the 'men who bed men' – the Greek word for those who take the active role. A passage in 1 Timothy also lists *arsenokoitoi* among the 'godless' who are 'contrary to the sound teaching that conforms to the glorious gospel of God'.[14]

But the message Paul proclaimed was one of freedom from that vast institutionalized idolatry and all that flowed from it. 'In the one Spirit,' he wrote to the Corinthians, 'we were all baptized into one body – Jews or Greeks, slaves or free.' 'There is no longer Jew or Greek,' he wrote to the Galatians, 'there is no longer male and female; for you are all one in Christ Jesus.'[15] There is that about the gospel of Jesus Christ that overturns the social structures of master and slave, owner and owned. It is not surprising then that St Paul should reject an ethic in which every sexual act was expressive of mastery and subordination. This leads him to his most daring and innovative statement about sex: 'the husband should give his wife her conjugal rights, and likewise the wife to the husband. For the wife does not have authority over her own body, but the husband does. Likewise the husband does not have authority over his own body, but the wife does.'[16] Paul takes the social platitude of the time (that the husband owns his wife's body) and turns it on its head by saying that the reverse is also true. Archbishop Rowan Williams remarks that these words 'carry a more remarkable revaluation of sexuality than anything else in the scriptures'.[17] They are a bomb under the entire sexual ethics that symbolized the mastery and subordination implicit in Roman culture. Sexuality, Paul here affirms, is a mutual act; an act in which partners encounter one another without the roles of owner and owned. This means that the penetrative role in sex is no more and no less symbolic of freedom and ownership than the receptive role: at a stroke, Paul revises the entire pattern of sexual symbolism that any Roman would have recognized and understood.

Paul's radical idea of Christian freedom obviously presented him with a dilemma. The ancient institution of slavery persisted, part of the social bedrock of the Roman empire. Neither Paul individually nor the young Church collectively could do anything in practical terms to put an end to it. So we find Paul addressing both Christian masters and Christian slaves and reminding them that whatever social structure might persist in the present dispensation, their Christian faith radically relativized it. Masters were to remember that they all had one master in heaven: that qualified their absolute freedom of action. Slaves, while going about their proper duties, were to do 'as for the Lord and not for men': that qualified their absolute lack of freedom. Paul makes it sufficiently clear that the institution of slavery – or rather the assumption of mastery by one human being over another – was part of the present 'age' that was soon to pass away. Within the body of Christ, on the other hand, we should already be experiencing something of the age to come, in which there is no longer Jew or Greek, slave or free, male and female.

As with the institution of slavery, so the Roman version of the institution of marriage persisted. Paul could no more undo that institution than he could abolish slavery. In the 'present age', husbands (even Christian husbands) continued to own their wives; and Paul's strategy, as in the case of masters and slaves, was to make them see how the gospel relativized and subverted the Roman concept of marriage, and how within the body of Christ they were to live as if in the 'age to come' in which there would be 'neither male nor female'. Paul's language frankly wavers between the innovative and the conservative, the radical and the acquiescent, and he is not consistent. But we owe it to him to take his most daring and challenging words as the standard by which to judge him; and judged by that standard Paul introduces a sexual ethic of radical equality.

Except that it wasn't Paul who introduced it. The seed of this radical revaluation of sexuality lies in the Lord's words about marriage and divorce. When Jesus said that men and women should not divorce each other, he gave us a hard saying that has caused much heartache and has elicited different pastoral responses from the Church at different times. What we must recognize is that instead of insisting on the law of Moses, which allowed husbands to divorce their wives but not the other way round, Jesus gave an equal right and standing to the wife.

In proposing a new sexual symbolism, derived from Jesus's own radical understanding of marriage and divorce, what meaning was Paul ascribing to the sexual act? Not the procreation of children, to which the later tradition of the Church ascribed the only legitimate use of the sexual act (echoing, as we have seen, that Old Testament imperative). The imperative for procreation has almost entirely vanished from the New Testament. Neither Jesus nor Paul discusses sex or marriage in terms of it. With the one exception of the story of Zechariah and Elizabeth, which is consciously modelled on Old Testament precedents and is part of St Luke's scene-setting for the birth of Christ, that powerful Old Testament shame and stigma for the barren woman has completely disappeared. So has the corresponding longing for immortality through one's descendents. Christians lived on the verge of the 'age to come': resurrection, not the perpetuation of the family name, was what occupied their minds and filled their horizons. Like Jesus, Paul was quite clear that the gospel required some to 'give up house or wife or brothers or parents or children for the sake of the kingdom of God'.[18] Paul is very pragmatic, both in his reasons for continence and in his reasons for marriage. He neither exalts virginity as an ideal, as later Christian tradition was to do; nor does he lay upon marriage a heavy duty of childbearing.

It is in the Epistle to the Ephesians that Paul (or the deutero-Pauline writer) comes close to ascribing a new symbolism for the sexual act. In marriage, he says, a man 'nourishes and tenderly cares for' his wife's body as if it were his own, and this, he says, is a 'great mystery' that signifies Christ and the Church. He doesn't say here what is implied in 1 Corinthians: that the nourishing and cherishing are mutual. The discussion does not move within the framework of radical equality of the Galatian and Corinthian letters, where 'there is no longer Jew or Greek, slave or free, male and female'. But the remarkable thing about the Ephesian passage is that it applauds sexual bodily delight as a gift in itself: not something justified in terms of pressing moral or civic or social duty, but just a gift, a thing of grace, and a reflection of the still greater and more gracious gift of Christ's love for his Church.

Paul's disapproval of homosexual acts in Romans and 1 Corinthians is inextricable from his negative judgement on the domination and subordination implicit in Roman society. All forms of human domination and submission are characteristic of a society that worshipped the created image instead of the Creator. The possibility of a sexual relationship between two men or two women that was *not* a part of that structure of domination and submission does not occur to Paul, just as it did not occur to anyone else. But the sketch in Ephesians of a new sexual symbolism in which two partners by their bodily delight reflect the love of Christ at least opens the door on the possibility that the same symbolism could be attributed to the bodily love of two people of the same sex.

But this glimmer of possibility was not followed up. The Church of later generations fell back upon the unexamined assumption that the prohibitions of Leviticus remained part of the gospel of Christ. There were moments when that assumption might have been challenged. At the beginning of the seventh century, we find St Augustine of Canterbury asking the advice of St Gregory the Great about pregnant women seeking baptism, menstruating women seeking holy communion, and men who have just had sex entering church. 'All these things', Augustine writes, 'the ignorant English need to know' (though it's obvious that Augustine felt he needed to know as well). Augustine supposed the answers to lie in Leviticus. Gregory was clear that what kept people from God was the flawed and wayward human heart, and he roundly tells him that fitness for the Christian sacraments is nothing to with the physical flow of blood or seed.[19] Yet Gregory did not pursue this radical thought: and his manual for bishops, *The Book of the Pastoral Rule*, reflects the now settled view of the Christian tradition that sexual intercourse is for procreation only.[20] Gregory was no more disposed radically to re-examine that aspect of the tradition than he was to question the propriety of slave boys being sold in the Roman forum.[21] Peter Brown points out that when the Church had the opportunity to press for the abolition of slavery in the fifth century, it failed to seize it.[22] And if Christian slave-owners were still defending their rights against the campaign of William Wilberforce and his friends in the nineteenth century, it is not fanciful to suggest that the teaching both of Jesus and of Paul about sexuality also carries within it implications which the Church has not yet fully properly appropriated or explored.

It is the contention of this chapter that the Church's long-standing antipathy to homosexual acts is rooted in culturally specific parts of the biblical tradition that do not provide grounds for a universal condemnation. The prohibitions of Leviticus are specifically to do with concepts of tribal purity, male dominance and racial survival, all of which belong to that

8

Are You My Friend?

We ended the first chapter with the words of St John's prologue, that those who receive the Word are born 'not of blood or of the will of the flesh or of the will of man, but of God'. The Word gives us a new identity: our earthly 'identities' – the race we belong to, or the kind of person our society deems us to be – are not determinative of what we are as God's children. It is the same truth that St Paul expounds in different words when he says that 'in Christ' we are no longer determined by our racial identity (there is neither Jew nor Greek) nor our social identity (there is neither slave nor free) nor our sexual identity (there is neither male nor female). These particular identities are the clothes we leave behind when we can put on our new identity of Christ. This is the principle of the narrow gate: the entrance so restricted that no baggage can be admitted. This must have been so much more evident to Christians in those centuries when every person brought to baptism was stripped naked before they entered the font, leaving their old identity behind them, and then, once baptized, was clothed in the new white robe of Christian dignity.

It has been the main theme of this study that Christians of most generations in the past have seen in the traditional idea of friendship one authoritative image for the way members of the body of Christ are related to Christ and to each other. As 'friends', we cannot take any final stand on race, country, culture or gender because in Christ we meet people whose race, country, culture and gender are different from ours, and yet in Christ we are 'friends' with them.

The image of friendship gives us some priorities for life in the body of Christ. We have no tools for shaping the life of the body of Christ other than those that are proper to friendship. The first characteristic activity of friendship is conversation. We noticed in the first chapter how the fourth evangelist makes conversation among the disciples part of his drama: it scarcely happens in the other Gospels, but here the disciples converse among themselves and with the Lord. Even after the bodily presence of the Lord is withdrawn, his presence in the Holy Spirit continues the conversation: 'when the Spirit of truth comes, he will guide you into all the truth'.[1] And the conversation is not with contemporaries only: we need a dialogue with our Christian friends in the past, for their perspective, while not necessarily better than ours, is illuminatingly different. Nor is conversation necessarily placid: robust debate is proper to friendship. Protest may be necessary, just as it is sometimes needed in friendship ('faithful are the wounds of a friend').

At least one half of every conversation is silence. So for the Church to be a society of friends it must listen to the Word. Here it is St Luke and not St John who gives us the dramatic interaction of Martha 'distracted with much serving' and Mary sitting at the Lord's feet and listening to his teaching.[2] Martha was too busy to sit and listen; but Mary did. She didn't need to speak; nor, maybe, did he. Friends do not need to talk to each other all the time. Archbishop Michael Ramsey, famous for long gaps in his conversation, once thanked a friend for his 'companionate silence'.[3] Such silences should mark the body of Christ quite as much as lively conversation.

The disciples in the Fourth Gospel, like Mary, hung on his words. 'Lord, to whom shall we go?' said Peter. 'You have the words of eternal life.'[4] 'The Holy Spirit,' says Jesus to them later on, 'whom the Father will send in my name, will teach you everything, and remind you of all that I have said to you.'[5] So the Church is the community of the Holy Spirit, hanging on the words of Jesus that the Spirit brings to our remembrance.

Sometimes there is a word for one disciple which is not meant for all, and that is an important part of the conversation of friends in the body of Christ. Take, for example, that unforgettable scene at the very end of the epilogue of the Fourth Gospel. Peter has had his private conversation with Jesus, who has asked him about his friendship and his love, and has spoken to him of his commission and his destiny. And Jesus sums up all he has ever said to Peter with the words with which they began their friendship all that time ago: 'Follow me.' And so they walk together, Jesus and Peter. But Peter turns and sees the 'beloved disciple' also following. 'Lord, what about him?' asks Peter. Jesus replies, 'If it is my will that he remain until I come, what is that to you? Follow me.'[6] Peter has been given his destiny, his path to walk. But he need not be told the destiny or the path of anyone else; not just to satisfy his curiosity. Of course, Peter and John (if John it be) have the same journey: they are on the way with Christ and to Christ. But their particular paths and destinies may differ, and that may be a proper secret between the Lord and each disciple.

This is a very powerful image that illuminates many aspects of life in the body of Christ. It speaks of each Christian having a particular vocation, a path that may differ in some respects from that of others. Yet that vocation is laid upon us by the Lord; we do not choose it for ourselves. Sometimes a word needs to be addressed to one person, which is not for everyone. Every priest in the confessional and every spiritual director knows the truth of this: there can be a word of advice, of gospel, which belongs to *that* person in *that* context, which cannot be generalized. Friendship accommodates this diversity of calling.

The story of Peter and the beloved disciple also speaks to us about the need for reticence within the body of Christ. 'What is that to you?' asks the Lord. Reticence is a proper part of friendship: good friends usually know when to speak and when to shut up, when to intrude and when to keep out, though of course even friends can sometimes get it wrong.

Aristotle took the view that you shouldn't have too many friends: friendship, for him, was a properly exclusive relationship. But what is so daring about the Johannine vision of the Church is that friendship is established between all who are followers of the Lord. There is, as so often, a twin truth here, and I think St John gives us both sides of it. All the disciples of Jesus are his friends: he has chosen them, loved them and asked of them the question, 'Are you my friend?' And yet, within the dramatic structure of the Fourth Gospel, there is one who is called 'the disciple whom Jesus loved'. As we have seen, there is a sense in which this unnamed disciple stands for all the rest: the image of the disciple reclining on the breast of Jesus belongs to the whole Church. But this unnamed 'beloved' disciple also reminds us of the particularity of love. We are particular and finite creatures, and with the best will in the world we cannot exercise equally the fullness of Christ's love towards all our fellow creatures. So we are not asked to turn our backs on the particularity of our relationships: our marriages, families, chosen friends. The body of Christ itself exists not only as a universal fellowship but as a local and particular one as well. There is a sense here in which race, country, culture and gender all find their way back into the exercise of Christian friendship: these are the particularities of our existence as John was particular to Jesus. We rightly divest ourselves of these particularities in baptism, but then the Lord gives them back to be our 'beloveds'. So we do have our own particular friendships, but our duty in the body of Christ is not to make them into cliques or exclusive coteries. We have a duty to make the whole of our church life something characterized by friendliness and hospitality and welcome. As the Bishop of Thetford has written:

> One of the things we need to recover within the Christian community is the beauty and value of friendships both between the sexes and between members of the same sex. Our churches should be communities of friendship – to stand against all the ways in which our modern patterns of life and

thinking push us into individualism and loneliness. We are made for fellowship, and whether in marriage or family, or in a life of celibacy or community, we need to find ways of dealing with the fact that it is not good to be alone.[7]

And here I return to those particular friendships which we have touched upon throughout this book: the friendship of two people of the same sex. We have explored some of the ways in which Christians in the past have lived quite comfortably with a whole range of different relationships, including same-sex friendships entered upon quite formally and sacramentally. Much of the custom and formality that attached to these friendships has been at times, as we have seen, indistinguishable from the ceremonies of marriage. With that wealth of history behind us, we should be glad to accept that two men or two women might enjoy a particular and committed friendship. We should be glad to respect the decision of two people to share a life together, or a home. We should be able to rejoice with those who seek to consecrate their friendship by prayer and sacrament. None of this is an innovation in the rich and varied history of the body of Christ. The wholehearted acceptance that such committed friendships might be as sexually expressive as those *other* committed friendships we call marriage – well, that would be a new chapter in the Church's dialogue with its own past. There are strong grounds, however, for seeing that as authentic development, not departure. In the preface to *The Friend*, Alan Bray movingly expressed the hope that the 'appropriation' of the past he described in his book might 'prelude a resolution of the conflict between homosexual people and the Christian church today'.[8] I echo the hope; but more than that, I hope that all Christians might rediscover something of the immense richness of our tradition of friendship.

'God is friendship,' wrote St Aelred of Rievaulx, reflecting on the eloquent image of the beloved disciple who reposes in the heart of God. In our particular friendships, we catch a glimpse of what it means to be friends with God. Perhaps we still have much to learn about the diversity of forms those human and particular friendships can take. In the meantime, the world is starved of friendship. That imposes on the body of Christ all the more of an obligation, and an urgency, to be a society of friends: friends of the Lord and friends of each other in him, and friends of the friendless who come in search of friendship.

Notes

1. I Have Called You Friends

1 John 15. 12–15.
2 John 1. 18.
3 John 15. 12.
4 1 John 3. 14 RSV.
5 2 John 7; 3 John 10.
6 John 1. 41.
7 John 1. 45.
8 John 11. 16.
9 John 12. 22.
10 John 11. 5.
11 John 13. 23.
12 John 19. 26.
13 John 20. 4.
14 John 21. 20–23.
15 Psalm 41. 7, 9.
16 Psalm 55. 12–14.
17 John 3. 19–21.
18 John 12. 2, 21–30.
19 John 13. 23; 19. 26–27; 20. 2; 21. 20.
20 John 18. 15.
21 John 1. 18.
22 St Thomas Aquinas, *Verbum supernum prodiens* (*English Hymnal* 330).
23 William Temple, *Readings in St John's Gospel* (Macmillan,

London, 1945), p. 404. Temple's translation; my modernization. See Temple's footnote on distinguishing *philia* and *agape* in this passage.

24 John 20. 11–18.
25 John 16. 7.
26 Erich Auerbach, *Mimesis: The Representation of Reality in Western Literature* (Princeton University Press, Princeton NJ, 1953), p. 41.
27 Cicero, *Laelius de Amicitia* 15, tr. J. G. F. Powell (Aris and Phillips, Warminster, 1990), p. 35.
28 John 1. 13.

2. Friendship and the Old Testament

1 Sirach 6. 5–13.
2 Sirach 6. 14–16.
3 Sirach 9. 10.
4 Sirach 22. 21.
5 Sirach 20. 16.
6 Sirach 41. 18.
7 Proverbs 17. 17; 18. 24.
8 Proverbs 19. 6.
9 Proverbs 27. 6 RSV. Compare Zechariah 13. 6: 'What are these wounds on your chest?' 'The wounds I received in the house of my friends.'
10 Proverbs 6. 24–27; 42. 7.
11 William Shakespeare, *Hamlet,* Act 1, Scene 3, lines 62–69.
12 Rudyard Kipling, 'If – ', *Rudyard Kipling's Verse: Definitive Edition* (Hodder & Stoughton, London, 1940), p. 576.
13 1 Samuel 18. 1, 3.
14 1 Samuel 19. 1.
15 1 Samuel 20. 16, 17.
16 1 Samuel 20. 41.
17 2 Samuel 1. 23, 25, 26.
18 2 Samuel 9.
19 P. Kyle McCarter Jr., *II Samuel,* The Anchor Bible (Doubleday, New York, 1984), p. 77.

20 See, for instance, E. W. Heaton, *Solomon's New Men: The Emergence of Ancient Israel as a Nation State* (Thames and Hudson, London, 1974), ch. 6.

21 Silvia Schroer and Thomas Staubli, 'Saul, David and Jonathan – The Story of a Triangle?' in Athalya Brenner (ed.), *Samuel and Kings: A Feminist Companion to the Bible* (Sheffield Academic Press, Sheffield, 2000), p. 22.

22 Isaiah 41. 8; see also the prayer of Jehoshaphat in 2 Chronicles 20. 7. It is these passages to which St James alludes when he writes that Abraham was 'called the friend of God' (James 2. 23).

23 Exodus 33. 11; but see also Exodus 33. 23.

24 Deuteronomy 34. 10.

25 See, for instance, Genesis 32. 30; Exodus 33. 23.

26 Wisdom 7. 27.

3. Friendship in the Classical Tradition

1 Philippians 4. 8.

2 Acts 17. 16–31.

3 Wisdom of Solomon 9. 1–2.

4 Plato, *Laws*, tr. Trevor J. Saunders (Penguin, Harmondsworth, 1970), p. 336.

5 Aristotle, *Ethics* 8.1, from *The Ethics of Aristotle*, tr. J. A. K. Thomson (Penguin, Harmondsworth, 1953).

6 Aristotle, *Ethics* 8.1.

7 Aristotle, *Ethics* 8.5.

8 Aristotle, *Ethics* 8.7.

9 Aristotle, *Ethics* 8.7. But in the *Symposium*, Plato describes the man who contemplates true beauty as 'attaining virtue, becoming immortal, and being the friend of God'.

10 Aristotle, *Ethics* 9.4.

11 Aristotle, *Ethics* 9.2.

12 Aristotle, *Ethics* 9.3.

13 Aristotle, *Ethics* 9.10.

14 Cicero, *Laelius de Amicitia* 18, tr. J. G. F. Powell (Aris and Phillips, Warminster, 1990).

15   Cicero, *De Amicitia* 20.
16   Cicero, *De Amicitia* 20.
17   Cicero, *De Amicitia* 44.
18   Cicero, *De Amicitia* 54.
19   Cicero, *De Amicitia* 64.
20   Cicero, *De Amicitia* 78.
21   Cicero, *De Amicitia* 89.
22   Powell in *De Amicitia*, p. 22.
23   Cicero, *De Amicitia* 15.
24   Powell in *De Amicitia*, p. 85.

4. St Augustine to St Aelred: A Developing Tradition

1   St Augustine, *Confessions* Bk 4, ch. 8 (13), tr. Henry Chadwick (Oxford University Press, Oxford, 1991).
2   Cicero, *Laelius de Amicitia* 97, tr. J. G. F. Powell (Aris and Phillips, Warminster, 1990).
3   St Augustine, *Confessions*, Bk 4, ch. 6 (11).
4   St Augustine, *Confessions*, Bk 6, ch. 14 (24).
5   St Augustine, 'Concerning Faith of Things Not Seen', 2, tr. A. W. Haddan, *Nicene and Post-Nicene Fathers*, vol. 3 (Hendrickson Publishers Inc., Massachusetts, 1994).
6   St Augustine, *City of God*, Bk. 19, ch. 8, tr. John Healey, ed. R. V. G. Tasker, Everyman's Library (Dent, London, 1945).
7   For St Basil and St Gregory Nazianzen, see Raymond Van Damm, *Families and Friends in Late Roman Cappadocia* (University of Pennsylvania Press, Philadelphia, 2003).
8   See Chapter 6 below on St Francis de Sales.
9   John Cassian, *Conferences* 16, ch. 2, *Works*, tr. E. C. S. Gibson, *Nicene and Post-Nicene Fathers*, vol. 11.
10   Cassian, *Conferences* 16, ch. 3.
11   Cassian, *Conferences* 16, ch. 6.
12   For all that follows on St Anselm, see R. W. Southern, *Saint Anselm: A Portrait in a Landscape* (Cambridge University Press, Cambridge, 1990).
13   Southern, *Saint Anselm*, p. 146.

14 Southern, *Saint Anselm*, p. 156.

15 Southern, *Saint Anselm*, p. 157.

16 Southern, *Saint Anselm*, p. 162.

17 In what follows on St Aelred, see Aelred Squire OP, *Aelred of Rievaulx: A Study* (SPCK, London, 1969), ch. 5.

18 St Aelred, *De Speculo Caritatis*, 3. 109–10; quoted in John Boswell, *Christianity, Social Tolerance and Homosexuality* (University of Chicago Press, Chicago and London, 1980), pp. 225–6.

19 Squire, *Aelred*, p. 111.

5. Sworn Friends

1 Pseudo-Dionysius, *The Ecclesiastical Hierarchy*, 7.3.11, tr. J. Parker, *The Works of Dionysius the Areopogite*, vol. ii, p. 161. The origins of sponsorship and godparenthood are described in Derrick Sherwin Bailey, *Sponsors at Baptism and Confirmation: An Historical Introduction to Anglican Practice* (SPCK, London, 1952).

2 John Bossy, *Christianity in the West 1400–1700* (Oxford, Oxford University Press, 1987), p. 15.

3 Alan Bray, *The Friend* (University of Chicago Press, Chicago and London, 2003), pp. 18–22, 36–8.

4 Bray, *The Friend*, p. 133.

5 Psalm 133. 1 (Vulgate Ps. 132. 1).

6 Bray, *The Friend*, pp. 241–6.

7 J. Wickham Legg, *English Church Life from the Restoration to the Tractarian Movement* (Longmans, Green and Co., London, 1914), p. 260.

8 Bray, *The Friend*, pp. 215–16.

9 R. W. Southern, *Saint Anselm: A Portrait in a Landscape* (Cambridge University Press, Cambridge, 1990), p. 148. See also Michael M. Sheehan, 'Christianity and Homosexuality', *Journal of Ecclesiastical History*, vol. 33, no. 3, July 1982, pp. 438–46.

10 Bray, *The Friend*, pp. 208–12.

11 John Boswell, *The Marriage of Likeness: Same-Sex Unions*

  in Pre-Modern Europe (HarperCollins, London, 1995), p. 220n.

12 Bray, *The Friend*, pp. 316–17.

13 F. Harris, *Transformations of Love: The Friendship of John Evelyn and Margaret Godolphin* (Oxford University Press, Oxford, 1988), p. 484.

6. Men and Women

  1 G. Vann OP, *To Heaven with Diana! A Study of Jordan of Saxony and Diana d'Andalo with a Translation of the Letters of Jordan* (Collins, London, 1960), p. 104.

  2 St Thomas Aquinas, *Summa Theologiae*, 2a 2ae, 23.1 (Blackfriars with Eyre and Spottiswoode, London, vol. 34: 1975; vol. 51: 1969), vol. 34, pp. 5–9.

  3 St Thomas Aquinas, Opuscula 8, *Compendium Theologiae*, quoted in Thomas Gilby (ed.), *St Thomas Aquinas: Philosophical Texts* (Oxford University Press, Oxford, 1951).

  4 Aquinas, *Summa Theologiae*, 3a 29.2 (1969), p. 65.

  5 St Thomas Aquinas, 'Commentary on Book 8 of the *Ethics*', quoted in Thomas Gilby (ed.), *St Thomas Aquinas: Theological Texts* (Oxford University Press, Oxford, 1955), p. 385.

  6 St Francis de Sales, *Introduction to the Devout Life*, ch. 19, tr. T. Barns (Methuen and Co., London, 1906), p. 252.

  7 St Francis de Sales, *Introduction*, ch. 19, p. 253.

  8 St Francis de Sales, *Introduction*, ch. 19, p. 254.

  9 St Francis de Sales, *Introduction*, ch. 19, pp. 258–9.

10 St Francis de Sales, *Introduction*, ch. 19, pp. 254–5.

11 J. Taylor, 'A Discourse on the Nature, Offices and Measures of Friendship, with Rules of Conducting it', *The Whole Works of the Right Reverend Jeremy Taylor DD*, ed. R. Heber (London, 1839), vol. 11. (1839), pp. 301–35.

12 Sir Thomas Browne, *Religio Medici*, Part 2, section 9, W. A. Greenhill, ed., (Macmillan, London, 1881) pp. 110–111.

13 J. Taylor, 'Rules for Married Persons' in *The Rule and Exercize of Holy Living* (New edition, Rivingtons, London, 1876), pp. 70–1.

14 F. Harris, *Transformations of Love: The Friendship of John Evelyn and Margaret Godolphin* (Oxford University Press, Oxford, 2003), p. 4.

15 The relationship is however treated sympathetically in F. Higham, *John Evelyn Esquire* (SCM Press, London, 1968), to which I am indebted for my first acquaintance with the story.

16 Harris, *Transformations*, p. 5.

17 Harris, *Transformations*, p. 6.

18 Taylor, *Holy Living*, p. 70.

7. Friendship and Homosexuality

1 For Hittites, Assyrians, Babylonians and Egyptians, see David F. Greenberg, *The Construction of Homosexuality* (University of Chicago Press, Chicago and London, 1988), ch. 4.

2 Greenberg, *Homosexuality*, p. 141.

3 Leviticus 18. 22.

4 G. A. Moore, *A Question of Truth: Christianity and Homosexuality* (Continuum, London, 2003), ch. 3.

5 Peter Brown, *The Body and Society: Men, Women and Sexual Renunciation in Early Christianity* (Columbia University Press, New York, 1988; Faber, London, 1989), p. 6; quotation from St John Chrysostom, *De Virginitate*, 14.

6 Brown, *Body and Society*, p. 25.

7 Greenberg, *Homosexuality*, pp. 185–9.

8 Greenberg, *Homosexuality*, pp. 184–5.

9 Ephesians 2. 15.

10 Cf. Brown, *Body and Society*, p. 10, 'Women . . . were failed males.'

11 Brown, *Body and Society*, pp. 29–30.

12 Romans 1. 26–27.

13 1 Corinthians 6. 9–10.

14 1 Timothy 1. 8–11.

15 Galatians 3. 28.

16 1 Corinthians 7. 3–4.

17 R. Williams, 'The Body's Grace' in C. Hefling (ed.), *Our Selves, Our Souls and Bodies: Sexuality and the Household of God* (Boston MA, 1996).

18 Luke 18. 29.

19 Correspondence preserved by the Venerable Bede, *Historia Ecclesiastica Gentis Anglorum, 1. 27; Bede's Ecclesiastical History of the English People*, ed. B. Colgrave and R. B. Mynors (Clarendon Press, Oxford, 1969), pp. 88–99; see also Brown, *Body and Society*, pp. 433–4.

20 St Gregory the Great, *Liber Regulae Pastoralis*, 27; *The Book of the Pastoral Rule and Selected Epistles*, tr. J. Barmby, *Nicene and Post-Nicene Fathers*, vol. 12 (Hendrikson Publishers Inc., Massachusetts, 1994), p. 57.

21 Bede, *Historia*, 2.1, pp. 132–5.

22 Brown, *Body and Society*, p. 23.

8. Are You My Friend?

1 John 16. 13.

2 Luke 10. 38–42.

3 Michael De-la-Noy, *Michael Ramsey: A Portrait* (Collins, London, 1990), p. 137.

4 John 6. 66–69.

5 John 14. 26.

6 John 21. 15–23.

7 David Atkinson, *The Message of Genesis 1—11* (Intervarsity Press, London, 1990), p. 73.

8 Alan Bray, *The Friend* (University of Chicago Press, Chicago and London, 2003), p. 6.

Further Reading

Aquinas, St Thomas, *Summa Theologiae*. Blackfriars with Eyre and Spottiswoode, London, vol. 34: 1975; vol. 51: 1969.

Aristotle, *The Ethics of Aristotle*, tr. J. A. K. Thomson. Penguin, Harmondsworth, 1953.

Auerbach, Erich, *Mimesis: The Representation of Reality in Western Literature*. Princeton University Press, Princeton NJ, 1953.

Augustine, St, 'Concerning Faith of Things Not Seen', tr. A. W. Haddan, *Nicene and Post-Nicene Fathers,* vol. 3. Hendrikson Publishers Inc., Massachusetts, 1994; originally published by the Christian Literature Publishing Company in the USA, 1887.

Augustine, St, *City of God,* tr. John Healey, ed. R. V. G. Tasker, Everyman's Library. Dent, London, 1945.

Augustine, St, *Confessions*, tr. Henry Chadwick. Oxford University Press, Oxford, 1991.

Bailey, Derrick Sherwin, *Sponsors at Baptism and Confirmation: An Historical Introduction to Anglican Practice*. SPCK, London, 1952. Three years later, Bailey went on to publish his ground-breaking book, *Homosexuality and the Western Christian Tradition* (Longmans, Green & Co., London, 1955).

Bossy, John, *Christianity in the West 1400–1700*. Oxford University Press, Oxford, 1985.

Boswell, John, *Christianity, Social Tolerance, and Homosexuality*. University of Chicago Press, Chicago and London, 1980.

Boswell, John, *The Marriage of Likeness: Same-Sex Unions in Pre-Modern Europe*. HarperCollins, London, 1995.

Bray, Alan, *The Friend*. University of Chicago Press, Chicago and London, 2003.

Brown, Peter, *The Body and Society: Men, Women and Sexual Renunciation in Early Christianity*. Columbia University Press, New York, 1988; Faber, London, 1989.

Brown, Peter, *Augustine of Hippo*. New edition, Faber, London, 2000, especially ch. 6.

Brown, Raymond E., *The Gospel According to John*. Geoffrey Chapman, London, 1971.

Brown, Raymond E., *The Community of the Beloved Disciple*. Paulist Press, New York, 1979.

Cassian, John, *Works,* tr. E. C. S. Gibson, *Nicene and Post-Nicene Fathers,* vol. 11. Hendrikson Publishers Inc., Massachusetts, 1999; originally published by the Christian Literature Publishing Company in the USA, 1894.

Chadwick, Owen, *John Cassian: A Study in Primitive Monasticism*. Cambridge University Press, Cambridge, 1950.

Cicero, *Laelius de Amicitia,* tr. J. G. F. Powell. Aris and Phillips, Warminster, 1990.

Greenberg, David F., *The Construction of Homosexuality*. University of Chicago Press, Chicago and London, 1988.

Harris, F., *Transformations of Love: The Friendship of John Evelyn and Margaret Godolphin*. Oxford University Press, Oxford, 2003.

Higham, F., *John Evelyn Esquire*. SCM Press, London, 1968.

Lewis, C. S., *The Four Loves*. Geoffrey Bles, London, 1960.

McCarter, P. Kyle, Jr., *I Samuel*, The Anchor Bible. Doubleday, New York, 1980.

McCarter, P. Kyle, Jr., *II Samuel*, The Anchor Bible. Doubleday, New York, 1984.

Moore, G., *A Question of Truth: Christianity and Homosexuality*. Continuum, London, 2003.

Plato, *Laws*, tr. Trevor J. Saunders. Penguin, Harmondsworth, 1970.

Plato, *Lysis,* or *On Friendship*, tr. W. R. M. Lamb, The Loeb Classical Library. Harvard University Press, Cambridge MA and London, 1925.

Price, A. W., *Love and Friendship in Plato and Aristotle*. Clarendon Press, Oxford, 1989.

Sales, St Francis de, *Introduction to the Devout Life*, tr. T. Barns. Methuen and Co., London, 1906.

Schroer, Silvia and Staubli, Thomas, 'Saul, David and Jonathan – The Story of a Triangle?' in Athalya Brenner (ed.), *Samuel and Kings: A Feminist Companion to the Bible*. Second Series, Sheffield Academic Press, Sheffield, 2000.

Southern, R. W., *Saint Anselm: A Portrait in a Landscape*. Cambridge University Press, Cambridge, 1990.

Squire OP, Aelred, *Aelred of Rievaulx: A Study*. SPCK, London, 1969.

Taylor, J., 'Rules for Married Persons' in *The Rule and Exercize of Holy Living*. New edition, Rivingtons, London, 1876.

Taylor, J., 'A Discourse on the Nature, Offices and Measures of Friendship, with Rules of Conducting it', *The Whole Works of the Right Reverend Jeremy Taylor DD,* vol. 11, ed. R. Heber. London, 1839.

Temple, William, *Readings in St John's Gospel*. Macmillan, London, 1945.

Van Damm, Raymond, *Families and Friends in Late Roman Cappadocia*. University of Pennsylvania Press, Philadelphia, 2003.

Vann OP, G., *To Heaven with Diana! A Study of Jordan of Saxony and Diana d'Andalo with a Translation of the Letters of Jordan*. Collins, London, 1960.

Williams, R., 'The Body's Grace' in C. Hefling (ed.), *Our Selves, Our Souls and Bodies: Sexuality and the Household of God*. Cowley Publications, Boston MA, 1996.

Index

Abraham 2, 14–15
Aelred of Rievaulx 29–32, 47, 69
Anselm 27–9, 39–40
Aquinas, Thomas 6, 44–6, 52
Aristotle 17, 19–20, 26, 29, 45, 52, 68
Atkinson, David (Bishop of Thetford) x, 68
Auerbach, Erich 7–8
Augustine of Canterbury 63
Augustine of Hippo x, 23–6, 29, 33, 47

Basil of Caesarea 25, 47
Beloved Disciple ('Disciple whom Jesus loved') 4–5, 31, 67–8
  see also John (Fourth Evangelist)
Blagge, Margaret, see Godolphin, Margaret
Bloxham, John 35–6, 39
Bossy, John 34
Boswell, John 39–43, 53

Bray, Alan x, 35–9, 41–3, 51–2, 69
Brown, Peter 55–6
Browne, Thomas 49, 63

Cassian, John 25–8, 32
Cicero 8, 17, 20–2, 24, 26, 29–30
Clanvowe, John 35, 37, 39
Crispin, Gilbert 28, 39

David 12–14, 21, 25
Diana d'Andalo 44
Dionysius, Pseudo- 33

Ecclesiasticus
  see Sirach, Jesus Son of
Evelyn, John 48, 50–1

Francis de Sales 46–8, 50

Godolphin, Margaret 48, 50–1
Greenberg, David x, 42–3, 53–4, 56

Gregory of Nazianzus 25, 47
Gregory the Great 63
Gundulf 28

Harris, Frances 49–51

Job 11, 15
John (Fourth Evangelist) 1–9,
    15–16, 30–1, 36–7, 47,
    64–8
Jonathan 12–14, 21, 25
Jones, Catherine 37
Jordan of Saxony 44–5
Judas Iscariot 1, 4–5

Kendall, Mary 37
Kipling, Rudyard 12

Lanfranc 27
Lazarus, Martha and Mary 4,
    47, 66
Leviticus 14, 54, 56, 63
Lewis, C.S. 2, 52
Lister, Anne 37–9
Luke 2, 4, 7, 66

McCarter, P. Kyle 13
Martha and Mary
    see Lazarus
Mary Magdalen 5, 7, 47
Moses 2, 14–15

Neville, William 35, 37, 39

Orestes 22, 24–5

Paul 2, 16, 30, 36, 54, 57–65
Peter 4–8, 36–7, 66–7
Plato 17–18, 26
Powell, J.C.F. 21–2
Proverbs 11, 15
Psalms 4
Pylades 22, 24–5

Ramsey, Michael 66

Schroer, S. 14
Shakespeare, William 12
Sirach, Jesus Son of
    (Ecclesiasticus) x, 10–11
Socrates 17–19
Southern, R.W. x, 28–9,
    39–43
Squire, A. 31
Staubli, T. 14

Taylor, Jeremy 48–9
Temple, William 6

Walker, Ann 37–9
Whytton, John 35–6, 39
Williams, Rowan 60
Wisdom of Solomon 15–16